CULTOGRAPHIES

T0326758

CULTOGRAPHIES is a new list of individual studies devoted to the analysis of cult film. The series provides a comprehensive introduction to those films which have attained the coveted status of a cult classic, focusing on their particular appeal, the ways in which they have been conceived, constructed and received,
and their place in the broader popular cultural landscape.
For more information, please visit www.cultographies.com

Series editors: Ernest Mathijs (University of British Columbia)
and Jamie Sexton (Northumbria University)

OTHER PUBLISHED TITLES IN THE CULTOGRAPHIES SERIES

THEY LIVE

D. Harlan Wilson

WALLFLOWER PRESS
LONDON & NEW YORK

A Wallflower Book
Published by
Columbia University Press
Publishers Since 1893
New York • Chichester, West Sussex
cup.columbia.edu

Copyright © Columbia University Press 2015

All rights reserved.

A complete CIP record is available from the Library of Congress

ISBN 978-0-231-17211-0 (pbk.)
ISBN 978-0-231-85074-2 (e-book)

Book design by Elsa Mathern
Cover image: *They Live* (1988) © Universal

CONTENTS

ACKNOWLEDGEMENTS

This book emerged from a place of primal fear and genuine wonder; I will always be grateful to the editors of the Cultographies series for giving me the opportunity to write it. I am also grateful to Wright State University-Lake Campus for the sabbatical from teaching that allowed me to perform the majority of my research. I want to thank my wife, too, for putting up with my antics and, as always, being my first and best reader.

For my daughters Maddie and Renee

THE BECOMING-PIPER

Two one-liners leap to attention like divining rods:

[1] 'I have come here to chew bubblegum and kick ass – and I'm all out of bubblegum.'

[2] 'Life's a bitch – and she's back in heat.'

Most twenty-first-century American teenagers probably don't know where these words come from, who speaks them, or what they mean. The source may even elude their parents. But something familiar – a sense of comic irony, a shiver of existential dread – echoes down the hallways of memory. In the real world, *déjà vu* is the limit. In *They Live*, the one-liners possess a special valence, signifying the alpha male pathology of the protagonist who utters them, Nada, as well as the alienating (and alien-infested) world he struggles to negotiate and disempower.

Likewise do the one-liners resonate on a meta-narrational level. Nada is played by former professional wrestling superstar Roderick Toombs, better known as 'Rowdy' Roddy Piper.

At the time of *They Live*'s release in 1988, he had reached the apex of a profitable career. Developments in cable television, pay-per-view, and the promotional efforts of media moguls Ted Turner and Vince McMahon had established professional wrestling as one of the most lucrative entertainment industries. In this pretend-battle 'sport', there are heroes, villains and characters who oscillate between moralistic poles. While he had moments of likability, Piper was almost always *bad*; racist, misogynistic, smart-mouthed and demented, his assholery seemed to have no boundaries. His role as Nada is comparatively tame to his role as professional wrestler, but the latter inevitably informs the former, and as the film progresses, we witness a distinct transformation in Nada from mild-mannered, lower-class, conformist American patriot to volatile, classless, individualistic American anarchist.

This transformation evokes Gilles Deleuze and Félix Guattari's concept of the becoming-animal, a complex process whereby one experiences a pathological metamorphosis, for better or for worse, sprouting the wings of angels or the fangs of werewolves and vampires; whatever the case, the process vies for agency. In *Kafka: Towards Minor Literature*, Deleuze and Guattari write: 'The becoming-animal effectively shows a way out, traces a line of escape, but is incapable of following it or making its own' (1986: 36–7). Many of Kafka's stories feature characters who change from humans into animals as a means of escape from oppressive patriarchal forces; the evolving physical body claws for a desired terminal identity. Nada experiences a similar crisis. Throughout *They Live*, he bears the cross of the becoming-animal, which is to say, of the becoming-*Piper*, a burden that culminates in his death as he 'shows a way out, traces a line of escape' for humanity. But it is through the act of becoming-Piper that the aforementioned one-liners exhibit a deeper resonance. To become Piper is to become violent, to become sexist and

2

hypermasculine – to become an American hero…

Of course, as a teenager growing up in 1980s Midwest America, idle theorisations escaped me. I thought Roddy Piper was cool. He had a cockiness and flair for mockery that my friends and I aspired to emulate. Our relationship was to some degree contingent upon the dynamism with which we ridiculed one another, as is often the case among teenage boys jockeying to establish a (masculine) sense of self. Piper served as a fine model. Other wrestlers came to prominence in the 1980s – Hulk Hogan, Ricky 'the Dragon' Steamboat, Jake 'the Snake' Roberts, the Honky Tonk Man, Randy 'the Macho Man' Savage, the Iron Sheik, Andre the Giant, Big John Studd, King Kong Bundy and Jimmy 'Superfly' Snuka, all of whom flaunted their own signature moves and personality traits. But none of them commanded our attention like Piper.

As with teenage boys, professional wrestlers assert identity by way of derision, and the sharper and wittier the derision, the better. Nobody could contend with Piper. At a height of 6'2" and an average weight of 180 lbs. in his early career (see Slagle 2000), he was smaller than most of his peers; linguistically, however, he towered in the sky like a mountain god. And he fought dirty. We liked that. We knew wrestling was fake – physically gruelling, but rehearsed and performative – and we knew wrestlers were actors. But that didn't stop us from losing ourselves in the drama of their counterfeit lives.

Piper's appearance in *They Live* only stoked my affection. The film was directed by one of my favourite filmmakers, John Carpenter, whose body of work consistently frightened and intrigued me from a young age. I saw my first Carpenter film in 1982 on my eleventh birthday. After enduring two month's of whining and pleading, my mother finally broke down and took me to my first R-rated feature, *The Thing*. I had never seen anything like it. The flailing tentacles, the buckets of blood, the boiling flesh, a *pectoralis dentata* that chomps off somebody's hands, a melted-off head that sprouts hideous insect legs – it fed my imagination to my detriment and benefit. In the years that followed, I became an ardent devotee of Carpenter, repeatedly devouring his movies at the theatre and on videocassette. Horror and science fiction movies like *Prince of Darkness*, *Escape from New York*, *Halloween* and *Big Trouble in Little China* opened up new realms of terror, adventure and insight for me. By the time *They Live* came out in 1988, I knew my Carpenter. I was sixteen and had been following the buzz for months. Trailers ran habitually on TBS, the television station based in Atlanta, Georgia, that in the 1980s boasted a virtual monopoly on professional wrestling broadcasts. Somehow I had even managed to acquire a promotional poster for the film, a considerable feat in the pre-Internet age for a Midwestern teenager from Grand Rapids, Michigan. It hung on the wall over my bed like a trophy. To clinch this spell of fanboyism, I even wore a 'HOT ROD' T-shirt to the opening night of the film, the same T-shirt worn by the wrestler/actor during 'Piper's Pit', an interview segment shown between matches in which Piper invariably belittled, suckerpunched and beat up his ostensibly harebrained interlocutors. I was not alone in my choice of clothing.

'Rowdy' Roddy Piper licks his chops as he taunts fans from the ring.

Needless to say, *They Live* exceeded my expectations. In retrospect, I realise that what I liked most about the film were its definitive cult elements. Over-the-top acting. Cheesy dialogue. Hyperbolic violence. Magic sunglasses. Gory alien faces. Wristwatches that open portals in the asphalt. A ridiculously long street fight that includes suplexes and body slams. And so on. These idiosyncrasies drew me to Carpenter's oeuvre in the first place. It reminds me just how much a cult aesthetic stems from male adolescent imagination and desire. That said, *They Live*'s social commentary didn't escape me, partly because that commentary is egregious, mainly because of the culture of fear and paranoia I had witnessed growing up during the climactic years of the Cold War.

At school, at home, at the movies and on TV, a message was drilled into me: Russians are evil communists and they're going to nuke the planet. First, though, communism will infect America like a virus, rendering us Orwellian zombies at best … This kind of mania made *They Live* as entertaining as it was chilling. The antagonists in the film are evil *capitalists*, but the theme of social and psychological invasion and control allied the aliens with the Russians – and the Cubans, who, in the wake of the failed Bay of Pigs invasion in 1961, an effort to oust Fidel Castro from power, remained a fertile communist threat, if only as a niggling reminder that *they lived*.

Two worlds coalesced for me in Carpenter's film: the real world of impending nuclear apocalypse, and the fictional world of professional wrestling with Piper in the catbird's seat. Both were 'rowdy'. And both interpellated me. Listening to inspiring songs on my Sony Walkman – ranging from R.E.M. to Iron Maiden – I envisioned myself in the effigy of Piper trouncing the Russians with arsenals of everything from flying kicks and atomic drops to machine guns and hi-tech cyberware. The event that unfolded on my mindscreen belonged to a cult film, and I was the star, an increasingly fluid becoming-Piper who dispatched the enemy *en masse*, saving humanity from extinction and preserving the moral economy of American capitalist life. As Deleuze and Guattari might say, I engaged in the same project as Nada, using the fantasy-agency of the becoming-Piper to 'show a way out' and 'trace a line of escape' from a matrix that I could not free myself from via my own volition and fortitude. This fantasy-agency allowed me to both cope with the looming horrors of the real while experiencing the real as a source of solipsistic *jouissance*.

They Live remains Roddy Piper's best film. Since then, he has continued to wrestle and act, making bottom-of-the-barrel Z-movies and TV shows, with some exceptions, such as a 2009 appearance in the raunchy American sitcom *It's Always Sunny in Philadelphia* as an over-the-hill wrestler named 'The Maniac'. I met him in 2008, twenty years after the release of *They Live*, at a horror convention in Maryland. I was promoting a new novel and Piper was a celebrity guest. Dressed in a dark blue jumpsuit, he hunched over a table in the dealer's room signing pictures of himself in movie and wrestling stills. He is old and weathered now, vaguely punch-drunk, and walks with a slight limp. We made small talk, and then I told him in some detail about the Cultographies title I had been commissioned to write on *They Live*. He listened patiently, made a frog face, and asked if I wanted him to sign anything. Getting an autograph hadn't occurred to me, but I snatched a photo of Nada from the table and handed it to him.

I felt a sort of light-hearted dismay when I noticed that Piper was chewing bubblegum.

As he scribbled down his signature, I remembered how different things had been in the 1980s. Piper and I – my *idea* of Piper and I … we were different people, with different bodies, desires and self-concepts. The world we live in had changed, too, plagued by the spectre of global terrorism and new breeds of racism, misogyny and systems/screens of control … Then it occurred to me that things weren't so different. They were simply extended, extrapolated, more aggressively televised, *mediatised* … Architectures of violence remain firmly erect. All that has changed are techniques of infliction, which evolved from the torrent of media technologies that exploded in the 1980s. For me, *They Live* not only marks the end of an era, but the beginning of a dangerous and exciting technological future. This is not surprising for a cult film clearly aware of itself as such. Contrary to popular belief, cult cinema, perhaps more than any other form, has been reliably *defined* by social, cultural and political critique. *They Live* certainly navigates this terrain. It is Carpenter's most politically charged film – a token example of cockeyed entertainment, yet also a critical attack on a world that, in the director's words, is 'fucked beyond belief, but it's the best there is' (quoted in Boulenger 2001: 44).

1

THE CULT OF THE EIGHTIES

REAGANISM

The 1980s began as a hopeful period in the United States. Americans anticipated a return to the romanticised prosperity and 'moral values' of the 1950s that were trampled during the 1960s and 1970s. Stephen Feinstein explains:

The decade of the 1980s in the United States was a very different time. ... The social upheavals in the 1960s brought about by the Vietnam War and opposition to it continued into the 1970s. Americans in the 1970s also witnessed the sorry spectacle of the Watergate scandal and President Richard Nixon's resignation from office. And the 1970s ended with the humiliating episode of Americans being held hostage in Iran. By 1980, it was time for a change. Americans were tired of political protests. They were eager to feel good about themselves and their country again. Sensing their mood, Ronald Reagan campaigned for president on the theme of renewing good feelings about America. (2006: 5)

These feelings belonged mainly to right-wing conservatives for whom Reagan functioned as the ultimate posterboy, if not saviour. 'For those happily on the right, the election of Reagan was evidence not that the next stage of decline had been reached but the point at which the liberal sixties might finally be expunged from national memory' (Thompson 2007: 9). Reagan implied such a turnaround in his physical stature as much as his ideology, policies and personal history. With wisened good looks, thick, immaculately groomed hair and a confident white smile, all set atop a dark, broad-shouldered, conservatively tailored two-piece suit, he conveyed an image of entrepreneurial masculinity – strong, wealthy, patriarchal, capable of guiding the nation to utopia. Sometimes he swapped the suit for jeans, a denim shirt, cowboy hat and boots, a fashion statement that connected him more intimately with American history and the wilderness that men dressed like him colonised and 'conquered'.

Hollywood stardom further reified Reagan's American-made image. Beginning in the late 1930s, he appeared in scores of films and television shows before turning to politics and becoming governor of California in 1967. As a child watching his State of the Union addresses – or rather, watching my parents watch the addresses – I knew he had been a famous actor. But my only frame of reference was *Bedtime for Bonzo* (1951), a comedy where Reagan's character attempts to educate a chimpanzee using 1950s child-rearing methods in order to prove that nurture, not nature, is what constructs identity. I don't recall seeing the film. I have vivid memories of media imagery featuring Reagan with a monkey, imagery that may have been circulated by democrats in order to undermine him, or at least make him look funny, during his two presidential campaigns. Notwithstanding *Bedtime for Bonzo*, the actor-cum-politician's celebrity status enhanced his appeal, fuelled by the pathological rigor of American image-culture. 'Reagan's presidency [was] the natural political counterpart to an eighties culture driven, and dominated, by the production and circulation of the image' (Thompson 2007: 4–5). Reagan's 'celebridency' was advanced even more by 'a use of cinematic references and clichés in order to secure his political legitimacy' (Thompson 2007: 99) – a curious case of rhetoric constituting image.

The president's religious beliefs coincided with his economic policies. Bourgeois, Christian, white, right-wing and republican – much like George W. Bush in the 2000s – Reagan favoured the rich, affiliated himself with neo-Christian morality and pitted America against a foreign nemesis, cultivating the notion that the nemesis would soon infect and annihilate America ideologically, economically and actually.[1] Taking all of these factors into consideration, the analogy between Reaganism and *They Live* is overt and resolute; without this president, I seriously doubt the film ever would have been made, at least in its current form as a critique of class divisions and capitalist power. If nothing else, the aliens represent what Kenneth Jurkiewicz has referred to as 'the implacable forces of rampant, merciless Reaganomics' (1990: 35). While this is perhaps the most important cultural signifier in *They Live*, the 1980s reflects a much wider spectrum of influence.

BIG HAIR

In the twenty-first century, the phenomenon of Big Hair is often 'blamed' on the 1980s. But it has recurred as an intoxicating vogue for centuries. Consider the fashion craze in the seventeenth century sparked by Louis XIV of France, who began to wear loud, lavish wigs to conceal the spectre of impending baldness (see Kwass 2006: 642). In the next century, French *maîtresse-en-titre* Madame de Pompadour gave life to the notoriously tall hairdo of the same name. And later, in the nineteenth century, American freakshow magnate P. T.

Los Angeles hair metal band Nitro outfitted in signature Jurassic bouffants.

Barnum turned Big Hair into literal spectacle with his 'Circassian Beauties', orientalised women made to look foreign and exotic by flaunting great wigs (see Thomson 1996: 249–50)

Big Hair holds a privileged position in postmodern memory, however, and unlike these localised examples, its thoroughbred emergence in the 1980s denotes a widespread social and cultural formation. For me, it symbolises the colourful modes of excess and abandon that distinguished the period, ranging from Reagan's socioeconomic policies to, say, the antics of rockstars (and rockstar wannabes) as depicted in *The Decline of Western Civilization, Part II: The Metal Years* (1988). Shot between 1986 and 1988 by Penelope Spheeris and released the same year as *They Live*, Big Hair abounds in this documentary of the Los Angeles glam-rock scene and its culture of reckless substance abuse, idiotic delusions of grandeur, and rampant egomania and squandering. Of course, such behaviour – and the hair that signified it – was not limited to Los Angeles. Nor was it limited to music scenes.

EXCESS

American excess became a moral obligation in the financial world, leading up to the stock market crash of 1987. Prior to the 1980s, 'US stock trading was in a state of depression' yet 'between 1980 and 1988, 25,000 merger and acquisition deals were completed, worth a total of $2 trillion' (Thompson 2007: 10, 11). Truly this phase is enframed by the guiding proverb of arbitrageur Gordon Gecko in Oliver Stone's *Wall Street* (1987): 'Greed is good.' But reservoirs can only hold so much water, and eventually they go dry. A hearty disavowal of reality thus authorised the fiscal life of 1980s America, particularly among the wealthy, who were empowered/deluded by Reagan's 'no-holds-barred form of capitalism' (Boozer 2007: 168). This mindset led to a number of economic woes. Inflation spiked early in the decade, setting the scene for the savings and loan scandal and an engorging national debt, both of which reached a climax at the end of the decade.[2] These instances of pecuniary Big Hair widened the gap between rich and poor, inciting a kind of Marxist sentiment in the latter. This sentiment manifests palpably in *They Live*. The film endorses the call-to-arms of the 'Communist Manifesto': proletarians must rise against and quash their bourgeois masters with an eye to accomplishing class equality in the not-too-distant future. Violence paves the way to class equality.

Nada is a symbolic prole who, in the end, uses violence to single-handedly overthrow the alien bourgeois capitalists by exposing them for what they are. More specifically, he uses the force of his masculine body to expose their grotesque, inhuman bodies and incite mass hatred for them. *Ideology stems from the flesh*.

MASCULINITY AND THE BODY

Big Hair is a telling extension of the body. An even more resonant symbol for this sort of cultural hyperbole is the body itself, especially in media representation and cinema, where an excessive masculinity rapidly came to prominence. Any form of excess produced by the human subject is a compensatory effect of some traumatic kernel; when threatened, masculinity bucks and flares, vying to reassert power and control in the social matrix. Constance Penley and Sharon Willis argue that masculinity is 'both theoretically and historically troubled', and in the 1980s, 'under the pressure of feminism and gay politics, and as a result of the demands of advanced capitalism for new kinds of workers, men [were] being asked to respond as men in new and different ways' (1988: 4–5). Coupled with the imminent threat of Soviet takeover and nuclear disaster, these crises of class and gender spawned new modes of action and representation for maleness, modes that took shape on the growing variety of data screens that increasingly defined the daily lives of urban and suburban Americans.

In cinema, the epitome of the übermasculinised body surfaced in the audaciously muscled action heroes portrayed by Arnold Schwarzenegger and Sylvester Stallone, movie stars who dominated the Hollywood blockbuster market. Prior to becoming an actor, Schwarzenegger almost single-handedly popularised the sport of bodybuilding; the culmination of his rise to fame can be seen in *Pumping Iron* (1977), a documentary of the 1975 Mr. Olympia and Mr. Universe contests. Thereafter he turned to acting, and just a few years later, he commanded the science fiction and fantasy genres with films like *Conan the Barbarian* (1982), *The Terminator* (1984), *Predator* (1987) and *The Running Man* (1987). Stallone appeared in action-packed cop, war and boxing dramas, most prominently the *Rambo* and *Rocky* franchises. The religiously glossy, overinflated, supersculpted physiques of each actor became fetishistic objects of desire – ironic silage for the male gaze, which had formerly eroticised the female cinematic body. Brian Caldwell writes:

Rock-hard insignias of Hope under the threat of phallic apocalypse.

Schwarzenegger's body has ... been described by one critic as 'a condom stuffed with walnuts', whereas Stallone ... has been referred to as Fenimore Cooper's 'leatherstocking on steroids'. More significantly in terms of filmic representation, Gaylyn Studlar and David Desser refer to Stallone's 'glistening hypermasculinity' as John Rambo and note how this 'emphasized in the kind of languid camera movements and fetishizing close-up usually reserved for 'female flashdancers'. (1996: 134)

In this era of Big Hair, Big Money and, ultimately, Big Fear and Paranoia, the male gaze turned inward, onto the male form, jacking it into phallic spectacle. Desire shifted from the sumptuous feminine (as exhibited by actresses such as Brigitte Bardot, Natalie Wood and Farrah Fawcett) to the Stallone/Schwarzenegger monster-hero – monstrous because of its hyperreal stature (made possible by anabolic steroids and human growth hormones[3]), heroic because of its infliction of violence upon terrorist forces.

By way of image and brutality, Stallone/Schwarzenegger assuaged a national anxiety incited by Reagan's Cold War America. *Rocky IV* (1985) emboldens this dynamic. Shot midway through Reagan's presidential career during the height of the Cold War, the film tells a clear-cut tale of good and evil. Stallone-Rocky represents the adamant, unshakable and moral (if dull-witted) American subject. Equally muscled and gleaming in the ring, Dolph Lundgren plays Ivan Drago, metaphor for the machinic, soulless, Orwellian Russian subject. Any critique of Reaganism is veiled at best; the simplistic narrative fails to problematise either half of the good/evil binary. Still, the film serves its purpose: not only does Rocky defeat Drago in the climactic match held in Moscow, the Russians are wooed by his mettle and grit, and before he knocks Drago out, they start chanting his name. *Rocky IV* culminates with a short motivational speech by the winner in which he implores everybody to get along, saying, 'If I can change, and you can change – everybody can change.' The film dispels the Cold War with blockheaded politics … but it dispels nonetheless.

While not as chiselled, oiled, and hyperreal as the benchmark Stallone/Schwarzenegger, Roddy Piper's body-image stands out in *They Live*; lean, hard and donning a mullet hairdo reminiscent of Stallone-Rambo, he signifies the masculine spectacle and desire of the 1980s. Whether Carpenter intended it or not – although he probably did, given his penchant for satire and burlesque – Piper-Nada extrapolates Stallone/Schwarzenegger, parodying their roughneck personas and critiquing them as sites of power and agency. Consequently Piper-Nada is a simulacra, a copy of a copy – what Jean Baudrillard would call the 'desert of the real itself', cast in the mould of our mediatised and image-obsessed desires (1981: 1).[4] This reference is apt: Baudrillard achieved cult status in the 1980s, theorizing postmodern consumer-culture and the eclipse of the self by the technocapitalist sign.[5]

Unlike Stallone/Schwarzenegger's films – with the exception, perhaps, of the ontologically and metaphysically playful *Total Recall* (1990) – *They Live* puts heavy emphasis on the hyperreal nature of Piper-Nada and the world(s) that he inhabits. And unlike *Rocky IV*, *They Live* critiques Reaganism with extreme prejudice. This critique is important to the Baudrillardian arc of the film in that Reagan himself becomes yet another instance of hyperreality, as Mike Dubose suggests: 'Reagan's renegade/cowboy image effectively blurs the real political relationship between central authority, morality, and mainstream values not just for the president but for Reaganism in general' (2007: 917).

BLOCKBUSTERS

Reagan's hyperreal media-image operated in a similar way to the media-images of Stallone/Schwarzenegger: an instance of compensatory excess that placated male anxiety under the aegis of prospective doom. These cinematic bodies gestured towards a viable agency. With the blockbuster film, excess took the form of cinema itself, further reifying the social, cultural and economic abandon of the era. A representation *par excellence* of the excess that I have discussed up to this point, the blockbuster culls together pathologies and obsessions with body-image, capital and media technologies.

In the abstract, blockbuster films exhibit three Big features: production budgets, special effects and box office returns. In *Blockbuster: How Hollywood Learned to Stop Worrying and Love the Summer* (2004), a reference to Stanley Kubrick's film *Dr. Strangelove, or, How I Learned to Stop Worrying and Love the Bomb* (1964),[6] Tom Shone writes:

> Once a purely economic term, with no generic prefer-
> ence, it was conferred solely by a movie's box office re-
> turns – and, by default, the audience. Thus *The Sound of
> Music* was a blockbuster [as was] *Fiddler on the Roof*
> and *Kramer vs. Kramer*. Today, it has – to paraphrase Julie
> Andrews – become the name a movie calls itself, be-
> fore it is even out of the gate. … Now, it signifies a type
> of movie: not quite a genre, but almost; often science
> fiction but not necessarily; something to do with action
> movies although not always. (2004: 28)

Shone locates the origins of the multifaceted (if generical-
ly vague) blockbuster in the films of Steven Speilberg and
George Lucas, namely *Jaws* (1975) and *Star Wars* (1977),
although their work in the 1980s solidified the form. Previ-
ous critics denounce the filmmakers for dumbing down the
movie industry.[7] Shone focuses on the ways in which they
innovated and revolutionised the industry. It's impossible to
deny the boyish appeal of such 'high concept' fare exempli-
fied by 'stylish and slick production qualities' and 'straight-
forward and easily categorized characters and familiar plots
that could be described briefly' (Thompson 2007: 97). This
was a momentous shift from the auteur filmmaking of the
1970s – 'scrappy, a little ragged, open-ended, ironic, ambiguous, often despairing' (Prince 2007: 8) – even if the 1980s
did not forsake auteurism altogether. But superficial glitz significantly displaced narrative depth. Guy Debord's theory of
the spectacle as 'a social relationship between people that
is mediated by images' (1967: 12) powerfully resounds in the
blockbuster.[8] Blockbusters not only changed movies; they
changed the way we think about movies (as representations)

and our relationship to movies (as represented subjects). Put differently, they taught us *not* to think, but rather to sit back and let movies do our thinking for us. 'In general, film in the 1980s was less politicized from an oppositional, even radical, perspective, and its style was lusher, glossier, and much less ironic and ambiguous than it had been in the late 1960s and early 1970s' (Prince 2007: 8).

THE IMPLODED AUTEUR

In the popular imagination, the auteur is an avant-garde film-maker, loosely speaking – an *artiste* of celluloid – an elitist, unconventional, subversive, uncompromising visionary. This depiction certainly applies to some filmmakers. Robert Cumbow reminds us that the auteur theory 'was never a theory at all but merely a policy defining the approach of certain film critics' (2000: 1). Hence the auteur is the auteur because the film critic says so – unlike, incidentally, the cult films produced by many so-called auteurs, which are cult films because the fan(atic) says so. The concept of auteur theory came to prominence in French cinema during the New Wave period in the 1960s, initially endorsed by director François Truffaut in his 1954 essay 'A Certain Tendency in French Cinema',[9] and eventually coined by film critic Andrew Sarris in his 1962 essay 'Notes on the Auteur Theory'. There have been shifting modes of emphasis and signification over the years. A bone of contention arose regarding the role of the director as an authorial god whose machinations invalidate the contributions of screenwriters and other sources of creative input (e.g. producers and cinematographers). In a 1971 review of *Citizen Kane* (1941), for instance, Pauline Kael challenged Sarris's ideas about the supreme authorship of the director, arguing that authorship is a collaborative process between the director and multiple parties. More recently, David Kipen annulled directorial primacy in *The Shreiber Theory* (2006), granting the spoils of authorship to the screenwriter. Sarris's ideas have been further problematized by developments in literary theory such as New Criticism, which sacrificed authorial intention in the name of textuality (i.e. the product of the author is all that matters). Despite these variations in perspective, however, it seems that the auteur is generally perceived as a director who has creative control over the writing, direction and production of his or her film.

John Carpenter, who 'often works on the scripts, editing and electronic music for his films, is clearly an auteur in the classic sense of the term' (Grant 2004: 10). Carpenter is in fact notorious for auteuristic mischief, repeatedly frustrating (and frustrated by) production companies and studio systems throughout his career.[10] He carved out a niche typified by this frequently cited interview comment: 'In France, I'm an auteur; in Germany, I'm a filmmaker; in England, I'm a genre director; in the U.S., I'm a bum' (quoted in Foundas 2008). Of course, Carpenter is all of these things. His filmography exhibits characteristics of what might be anticipated from such varied perspectives.

In principle, the auteur and the blockbuster filmmaker are diametrically opposed breeds. One makes movies to make 'art', per se, and the other makes movies to make money. Both aspire to 'entertain' viewers. Carpenter's auteurism has been called 'a search for – and confrontation with – new order, in the same sense that all art is an effort to reorder the universe, or at least one's vision of it' (Cumbow 2000: 2). Most if not all auteurs undergo a similar journey, 'forging a vision out of bullshit' (Boulenger 2001: 33). Carpenter has made movies for big and small screens, for powerhouse companies and indie studios, and with high and low budgets. Whatever the context, most of his work romanticises the blockbuster form; he really wants to be a blockbuster filmmaker, but on his own conditions, in accordance with his own ethics, desires and codes. Regarding the content (i.e. a use of special effects and elements of fantasy and science fiction), his 1980s films had a lot in common with blockbusters like *The Empire Strikes Back* (1980), *Raiders of the Lost Ark* (1981), *E.T.: The Extra-Terrestrial* (1982), *Return of the Jedi* (1983), *Ghostbusters* (1984), *Back to the Future* (1985) and *Batman* (1989). His inability to garner the ratings of these films wasn't for lack of funding; according to the *Internet Movie Database*, the production budget for *The Thing* (1982), for example, was $15 million, as opposed to $10.5 million for *E.T.* that same year. On the contrary, Carpenter's narrative structure distinguished his movies. He did not kowtow to conventional, expected or accepted narrative formulas – *especially* vis-à-vis the blockbuster formula, which is ideally accessible to all ages and intended for 'family fun'. Carpenter's cult cinema demonstrates wilful 'failures' to manifest blockbusters and the sizes of audiences that flock to them. In effect, his cinema can be viewed as a metafictional critique of the blockbuster, exposing its prescription and inscription of desire onto the social body. He is what we might call an imploded auteur, blurring the boundaries between blockbuster and cult productions.

CODA: THEY LIVE

In addition to metafictional undertones and genre blending, dominant elements of Carpenter's cult cinema (and cult cinema in general) include excessive gore; rampant intertextuality; nostalgia for real and filmic histories; attitudes of rebellion towards the processes of filmmaking, storytelling and representation; B-movie 'badness'; and political bearings that expose the insecurities and idiocies of mass culture and nexuses of (capitalist) power. Broadly speaking, Ian Conrich and David Woods write:

Carpenter is … one of a group of key filmmakers who came to be associated with the horror new wave of the late 1970s and the early 1980s … the audience that grew up with his films at the dawn of the video age. For such an audience Carpenter is often seen as a director of cult films […] A B-movie aesthetic of sensationalistic, uninhibited and confident genre filmmaking has continually been a mark of Carpenter's productions. (2004: 3)

Influenced from an early age by monster movies like *King Kong* (1933), westerns such as Howard Hawks' *Rio Bravo* (1953), and above all science fiction like Jack Arnold's *It Came from Outer Space* (1953), Fred M. Wilcox's *Forbidden Planet* (1956), Roger Corman's *Conquered the World* (1956) and Val Guest's *Quartermass II: Enemy from Space* (1957) (see Muir 2007: 5–6), Carpenter, in retrospect, seemed destined for the realm of cult aesthetics. His work in the 1980s is the most animated, provocative and troubled of his cult canon: *The Fog* (1980), *Escape from New York* (1981), *The Thing* (1982), *Christine* (1983), *Starman* (1984), *Big Trouble in Little China* (1986), *Prince of Darkness* (1987) and finally *They Live* (1988). The subject of this title in the Cultographies series is not only a fitting coda for this decade-long filmography and the late Cold War era. An acid test for Carpenter's craft, *They Live* speaks inwardly, to itself and to the sibling films that preceded and succeeded it. Likewise does it speak outwardly, to the world at large, to America – not, as the US national anthem would have it, 'land of the free and home of the brave', but rather *land of the creed and home of the slave*.

2

WAKE-UP CALL

They Live derives from an eight-page illustrated story, 'Nada' (1986), which appeared in issue six of the comic book *Alien Encounters*. Ray Nelson's short story 'Eight O'Clock in the Morning' (1963), originally published in *The Magazine of Science Fiction and Fantasy*, served as the basis for 'Nada'. The comic was also written by Nelson and illustrated by Bill Wray, who is more well-known for his work in American comedy magazine *MAD* and the splattershtick cartoon *The Wren & Stimpy Show* (1991–98), both cult productions in their own right. As is often the case, the film and its sources are different narrative animals. 'Defined as a "wake-up call" by Carpenter at the time, *They Live* – a western disguised as a B sci-fi movie – proved that even with limited means, the director of *Halloween* was able to deliver both a challenging movie and a true ode to professional wrestling' (Boulenger 2001: 209).

'Nada' stays relatively faithful to 'Eight O'Clock in the Morning'. There are minor alterations, most of which have to do with Wray's visualisation of Nelson's prose. Unlike the far more plot-driven than detail-oriented story, the comic is archetypally noir – urban, shadowcast, übermasculine, oneiric, violent and hardboiled. Furthermore, the protagonist embodies the psychological condition of the noir hero: 'In film noir, the hero's penetration of the external labyrinth, the city, mirrors – often through a funhouse mirror – the transforming path he follows along his internal labyrinth. The farther outside himself he goes, the deeper he may find himself to be on the inside' (Christopher 1997: 18). In other words, the hero's descent into the labyrinth of the city mirrors his descent into his own psyche, which is as convoluted and treacherous as the city itself. So it goes with George Nada, whose descent from beginning to end constitutes a literal and metaphorical cycle of birth and death.

On the first page of 'Nada', a man stands on a dimly lit street corner in a trench coat, smoking a cigarette. Above him looms the proverbial Night City, an orderly and electric collision of skyscrapers beneath a starry dome. The man introduces himself – 'My name is George Nada. Nada is the Spanish word for nothing' (1986: 20) – and explains that a stage hypnotist awakened him.[11] Now he recognises 'the nonhuman faces, the faces of the Fascinators' (1986: 20), hideous pulp sci-fi monsters with constellated bug-eyes, gaping maws, yellow fangs and claws, and pink amphibious skin. Additionally, he sees and hears messages on signs, radios and TVs such as 'OBEY', 'MARRY AND REPRODUCE', 'WE ARE YOUR FRIENDS' (1986: 21). In this state of lucidity, Nada somehow understands that the Fascinators have been hypnotizing the human race, and he realises that he must not give himself away lest he return to a soporific, passive state. He receives an ominous phone call: 'This is your controller, Police Chief Robinson. Tomorrow at 8:00 a.m. your heart will stop!' (ibid.). The call sets the narrative quest in motion.

To annul the prophecy of his death, Nada determines to rouse other humans and revolt against the Fascinators.[12] In the process, he goes on a minor killing spree, brutally murdering Fascinators he encounters on the street and at the apartment of his girlfriend, Lil, a scantily clad, large-breasted *femme docile* who Nada beats up in an attempt to wake up. She remains in the dark, however, and Nada, losing his grasp of reality, ties her to the bed and hits the streets again, although not before arming himself with a glock from the neighbour's gun vault. At a bar he sees a Fascinator on TV repeating the phrase, again, 'WE ARE YOUR FRIENDS' (1986: 25), and he has an epiphany. He takes the subway to the TV station, blowing out the green brains of Fascinators along the way. The last Fascinator he kills is the TV announcer. The camera holds on the creature's gruesome, bleeding face, and from off-camera, Nada shouts this mantra: 'Wake up! Wake up! See us as we are and kill us!' (1986: 27). It works. 'The city heard my voice', he explains in the final caption, 'but saw the Fascinator's image, and the city did awake, and the war began' (ibid.). Unfortunately Nada doesn't live to fight another day. It is eight o'clock in the morning, and the last panels show his head gruesomely decomposing into a cracked skull, fulfilling the prophecy, and rendering him, 'once and for all, nada' (ibid.).

Noir aesthetic aside, Carpenter stays moderately true to the comic; he extrapolates it in some detail, tweaking and deepening its central themes. One stark difference is the look of the aliens, who are not bug-eyed monsters but more like zombies. I will discuss the symbolic resonance of this variation in a moment. Most noticeably, Carpenter's cinematic reproduction diverges from both 'Nada' and 'Eight O'Clock in the Morning' in its critique of 1980s American society and culture as well as its celebration of professional wrestling ethics and 'artistry', the latter of which have always combined hard-nosed drama with not-quite-slapstick comedy (although professional wrestlers essentially enact the pseudoviolent antics of the Three Stooges). At the same time, much of the humour of professional wrestling comes from its hyperdramatic stageplay, from the grave degree to which it takes itself seriously, or presents itself as taking itself seriously. Humour results from *dramatic excess*, making professional wrestling another fitting homebody for the 1980s, not to mention something that sits comfortably in a cult film.

The 'sport' gained slow popularity in the early 1970s and 1980s primarily via cable broadcasts on TBS, but it wasn't until promoter Vince McMahon established the WWF (World Wrestling Federation) in the early 1980s that it found a mass audience. In 1985, the first Wrestlemania, an annual pay-per-view event that remains alive in the twenty-first century, solidified the popularity of professional wrestling, and John Carpenter was among the mass of admirers. In 1987, he attended Wrestlemania III, met Roddy Piper and thought he would be a good fit for *They Live*, which was in the conceptual stages. Included in *Born to Controversy: The Roddy Piper Story* (2006) are clips from an interview with Carpenter where he explains: 'There's something about [Piper] that is unlike other Hollywood actors. He seems to have lived life. … After I got to know him, I thought, well, this is perfect. Let me give him a try in this role, because I think he has an enormous amount of talent, and he's very real. And he is John Nada, basically. That's kind of his life story.' Piper agrees, noting his affinity for Nada, 'a guy that wants to mind his own business and starts to run into all kinds of difficulties that nobody else is noticing. … He tries to correct it, and in correcting it, he has to blow away a few people. Ain't a lot of difference between John Nada and Roddy Piper.'

Initial shooting of *They Live* began in March 1988 in downtown Los Angeles. *Prince of Darkness* debuted five months earlier, in October 1987, and grossed over $14 million at the box office – nearly five times the cost of production – even if reviews of the film were tepid at best. Critics accused *Prince of Darkness*, the first in the Alive Films deal (see note 10), of hollow characterisation, narrative depthlessness and cheesy antics. In 1987, Roger Ebert, writing for the *Chicago Sun-Times*, concluded that it 'contains the ingredients for a much better movie', whereas Richard Harrington of the *Washington Post* said the film 'stinks' and is 'just after cheap thrills'. *Prince of Darkness* resonated with viewers and made money, however, and producers greenlighted a new film.

Carpenter received another $3 million to make *They Live*. Unlike *Prince of Darkness*, a complex amalgam of gothic horror and science fiction that recalls Edgar Allan Poe and H.P. Lovecraft, the second Alive Films instalment appears at first glance more one-dimensional, combining pulp western and science fiction in token shoot-'em-up fashion. But *They Live*'s 'comic book simplicity masks a network of deeply interlacing, sometimes conflicting, ideas and ideologies' (Cumbow 2000: 165). The promotional poster for the film calls attention to its depth of meaning and fundamental theme of (mis)perception. Eyes and eyewear are the focal points. This script runs across the top of the poster:

> You see them on the street. You watch them on TV.
> You might even vote for one this Fall.
> You think they're people just like you.
> You're wrong. Dead wrong.

Beneath the forewarning is Nada's exposed eye, dilated and wide with surprise, yet defined by a frowning brow. He has slid a pair of mirrored sunglasses down the bridge of his nose. One lens dominates the centre of the poster. Faintly garbled by lines of television static, the lens shows the full physiognomic reflection of a representative alien: bulbous insect eyes, two long rows of decayed horse teeth, hollow nose holes, metallic skull etched with raw red sinews and patches of

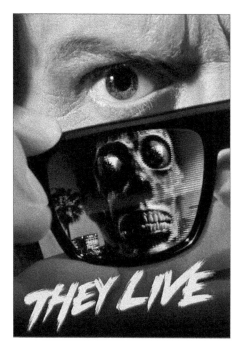

Nada perceives his enemy in the promotional poster for *They Live*.

blood. Behind the ugly mug is a hyperreal LA backdrop with a foreboding lava-coloured sky and the silhouette of a palm tree hanging over a distant, illuminated cityscape.

As we see in the film itself, the aliens/capitalists look like humans, if only upper-class humans (non-military males often wear business suits, females high-end dresses). Only by viewing them through the lenses of the sunglasses is Nada (and by extension the viewer) able to see their true faces. So technically the poster tells a lie. That is, it suggests their true faces are not *revealed through* but *reflected off* of the lenses, meaning that the alien/capitalist presumably standing in front of Nada can be seen *au naturel* without the glasses. We can attribute this inconsistency to the vagaries of marketing imagery. The poster nonetheless problematises perception and serves as an effective *reflection* of the ways in which the film problematises perception, literally and figuratively. We can even read the alien/capitalist in the poster as a metaphor for the viewer/consumer, for whoever is looking at the poster (and hence at Nada) and might purchase a ticket to see *They Live*. By this logic, the poster implicates the human (a potential buyer 'acting' within a capitalist matrix) as an alien, blurring the boundaries between self and other.

The bodies of the aliens reify this idea. They are not stock science fiction bug-eyed monsters or non-anthropomorphic organisms. Carpenter conceived of them as decayed zombies rather than the multi-eyed frogs of 'Nada' and 'Eight O'Clock in the Morning'. According to the production notes on the *Official John Carpenter Website*, 'make-up artist Frank Carissosa was responsible for implementing Carpenter's concept of the alien ghouls. Carissosa, who also worked on the Carpenter thriller *Prince of Darkness*, strove to create decomposition and menace in the ghouls, whose faces were made from latex cases and painted to resemble the last remaining remnants of human form.' Physically the aliens resemble semi-muscled human skeletons – that which lies beneath the skin. They are extra-terrestrials from outer space, but given their appearances and actions, the aliens collectively allegorise human desire, which manifests as capitalist energy and social economy.[13] They are the horrific potential (and underlying reality) that lurks beneath the human, quite literally: bone and blood, unmasked by the formality of flesh. Foregrounding the unbound visage of the alien in Nada's mirrored lens, the promotional poster does not immediately call attention to this dynamic and the relationship between desire and capitalism, but it does underscore the threat of perceptual construction that serves as the film's guiding theme and source of friction.

This is a theoretical concern. On the bare-knuckled surface, the poster ably represents Carpenter-label cult cinema with little sense of mystery or suspense: the gory, corny secret that Nada uncovers throughout the film is thrust in our faces, and viewers even remotely familiar with Carpenter's work up to this point know that they will be in for some kind of science fiction and/or horror artifice.

The near two-minute promotional trailer for *They Live* is somewhat less revealing. It exposes a warts-and-all alien only at the end, for a split second. Viewed through Nada's sunglasses, the alien wears a business suit and reads a newspaper at a kiosk on the street, then turns and looks at the camera – that is, at Nada and the viewer – its round, wide, white eyes projecting a sense of the Freudian uncanny from dark skull sockets. A roughly edited sequence of snippets and flashcuts leads up to this climactic shot. The aliens go unmentioned. As we jump from scene to scene, context to context, Nada and other characters explain: 'They're all about you … They're running the whole show … They are safe as long as they are not discovered … I don't know what they are, or where they came from, but we gotta stop 'em … They have us! Look at 'em – they're everywhere!' And so on. Interspersed throughout the trailer are screenshots of deep space onto which the word 'THEY', illuminated by a toxic blue corona, sails onscreen accompanied by the sound of a speeding aircraft and a low, monstrous growl.

The trailer gets more chaotic as we approach the end. Nada delivers one-liners and the narrative devolves into pyrotechnics and gunfire. Overall it is difficult to assess how effective or ineffective the trailer and the promotional poster were in generating sales for *They Live*, as is often the case with cinematic marketing imagery; based on the film's financial success, we can assume they played some role. They certainly piqued my interest, partly because of the content, partly because of the director – mainly because of Roddy Piper, my professional wrestling (anti)hero, who would be appearing in his first (and last) starring role in what I perceived to be a major motion picture event.[14]

3

REEL POLITIK

The first part of *They Live* is set in Justiceville,[15] a shantytown encampment situated on the periphery of downtown Los Angeles. Nada squats here with an eclectic group of other homeless people. As in the comic, the elegant skyscrapers of the cityscape loom over Nada and his cohorts in blight, but as part of the backdrop, accentuating the disparity between downtown wealth and fringe poverty. Carpenter filmed *They Live* 'on locations that bore the closest possible resemblances to the settings in the film; no studio set was used to create Justiceville or the old church or the flophouse on Skid Row' (*Official John Carpenter Website*). He did this to convey the greatest degree of verisimilitude not only for the physical landscape but for the class divisions they signified.

In a cosmopolitan city in one of the world's wealthiest countries, the disparity between economic classes is so distinct and widespread. There is more than a little irony in the fact that these places were so easily located in natural surroundings and this brings particular relevance to the story itself. Carpenter worked closely with his crew to create an air of grim reality around *They Live*. Standing on the outskirts of downtown Los Angeles at the Justiceville location, it is easy to imagine how shut out the real homeless must feel: the dramatic backdrop of high-rise office towers, freeway lights and air traffic contrast sharply with the shadowy hovels on the set. Much of the film was shot at night, which required Gary Kibbe, director of photography, to highlight the drama of each scene while working with a limited supply of light. (Ibid.)

They Live foregrounds the perspective of the homeless. This is essential to its narrative constitution and stems directly from Carpenter's personal experience.

'We went into the dirtiest alleys we could find', [Carpenter] recalls. 'The environment was very familiar to me. When I first came to California – lo these 20 years ago – to attend the USC film school, I lived in the ghetto. I went to downtown Los Angeles to go to all-night grindhouse movie theaters, where the winos slept. So, I knew about the pain and poverty of the homeless. But when I went back to downtown LA to shoot *They Live*, I was shocked to see how many *more* people live on the streets now. The problem has grown to *unbelievable* proportions'. (Quoted in Swires 1988: 38–9)

A sense of realism probably had something to do with *They Live*'s success among audiences. Critics were polarised, loving or hating the film for its overt B-movie badness. Pro-Carpenter critics acknowledged a clear meta-referential quality, an inherent filmic awareness and celebration of its own badness. Detractors rebuked Carpenter and his actors for being incompetent as well as trying (and failing) to make social commentary. In a *London Times* review, Sheila Johnston discusses the film with enthusiasm for its 'cheerfully cheesy' special effects and ode to cinematic kitsch. '*They Live* takes its tone from the Z-budget sci-fi of the 1950s, in which monsters were tracked down with a truly McCarthyite fervor. The dystopian sequences, shot in black-and-white, have a deliberately dated, Orwellian feel, with their authoritarian slogans and the old chestnut of subliminal conditioning' (1989). The *Washington Post*'s Richard Harrington, however, denounces the film for similar reasons:

> Even for sci-fi, the creatures-walk-among-us plot of *They Live* is so old it ought to be carbon-dated. Oh, sure, director John Carpenter trots out the heavy artillery of sociological context and political implication, but you don't have to get deep down to realize he hasn't a clue what to do with it, or the talent to bring it to life. It's much like the Carpenter-written music for *They Live* – a boring, bare-bones two-note bass riff masquerading as a soundtrack without ever approaching a resonant chord. (1988)

A certifiable Carpenter-hater, Harrington accuses the director of being cliché, whereas Johnston applauds him for it.[16] The difference is Johnston suggests he uses clichés for a calculated and successfully rendered purpose, as opposed to mere reckless idiocy. Put simply, she thinks Carpenter knows what he's doing and does it well.

In the end, the politics of *They Live* ensured modest success with viewers given the social climate of the year of its release. 'Distributed by Universal, *They Live* premiered shortly before Election Day 1988, and the timing was perfect. Since Carpenter's film was political in nature, it benefited from the political atmosphere. Was George Bush an alien? Was Dan Quayle? As a result of its humour and good timing, *They Live* was a box office hit' (Muir 2000: 40). Elected as president

Ronald Reagan: cowboy or alien?

and vice president in 1988, George Bush Sr. and Dan Quayle were the successors to the Reagan administration in which Bush Sr. served as vice president. The new Republican administration furthered its antecedent's policies. The question posed by *They Live*, however, speaks more to the recent past than to the near future: Was *Reagan* an alien? The figure of Reagan is vital to this context. As a movie star and symbolic 'cowboy' (i.e. conqueror of the American west as depicted in cinema), he belongs to the dream factory of Los Angeles culture, and his emergence as bourgeois father figure, patriarch, saviour and puppetmaster harmonises with the institution of the film's collective, covert antagonism. In this capacity, Carpenter's '*reel* politik' works most efficiently, coercing Americans to face the fears and desires evoked by the forces of a dubious hypercapitalist government. The film expresses what a lot of people were thinking but were afraid to say.

A so-called reel politik clinches *They Live*'s cult status and impacts many cult films. As Ernest Mathijs and Xavier

Mendik write in *The Cult Film Reader*, 'A common tool in the politically inspired cult film is that of deconstruction, of breaking down the cohesiveness of official culture by exposing its incoherencies and prejudices, and by celebrating "lapses, breaks and gaps" in its discourse' (2008: 10). They are not talking about Derridian deconstruction but rather new ways of seeing made possible by the elimination of objects of consciousness that have been socially constructed in the characters and the viewers, a task that Carpenter's film performs. A reel politik isn't enough, though – if the film merely served as a dramatically sanctioned and potent ideological pamphlet, it would be something else. This goes for films that fall neatly into popular speculative genres, cult cinema's default territory, and outside of them.[17] It was the combination of political commentary and enthusiastic schlock that secured *They Live*'s positive viewer reception. I will explore the variables of that schlock in the next chapter while analysing the narrative structure and aesthetics of what remains Carpenter's most allegorical film.

They Live did not meet with immediate commercial success. But it raked in $4,827,000 over its opening weekend (6–8 November 1988), almost $2 million more than it cost to make, and its final gross in the United States was $13,008,928 (*IMDb*). The film is an unequivocal cult articulation and it's difficult to believe that Carpenter might have expected better returns. Prior to the release of *They Live*, he admitted treading precarious waters. 'I recognize the danger … People who go to the movies in vast numbers these days *don't* want to be enlightened. My editor leaned over to me at a screening of *They Live*, and very softly said, 'This is different from your other films. This is a *message* movie.' I whispered back, 'Yeah, but don't *tell anyone*' (quoted in Swires 1988: 43).

Even though, like *Prince of Darkness*, *They Live* made money, the Alive Films deal fell through. It would be four years before Carpenter made another film, *Memoirs of an Invisible Man* (1992). This marked a return to major studio production (Warner Bros.), which meant a forsaking of the creative control that the director so deeply cherished, along with his distinctive cult élan, and he only took on the project after a fallout between star Chevy Chase and original director Ivan Reitman of *Ghostbusters* (1984) fame. The reason for the four-year gap: 'sheer creative fatigue' (quoted in Boulenger 2001: 214). He also wanted to devote more time to his young son and ill father. As for Alive Films, Carpenter says, 'I had a dispute with Universal at that time, so I didn't complete the movies I was supposed to have made' (ibid.). The nature of that dispute has never been disclosed, but it likely had to do with Universal's unceasing resolve to 'make it on the cheap' (quoted in Boulenger 2001: 216).

Memoirs of an Invisible Man crashed and burned at the box office.[18] *They Live*, on the other hand, did quite well and commands an 83% critical rating on *Rotten Tomatoes* in comparison with *Memoirs of an Invisible Man*'s paltry 23%.[19] A premier online aggregator of contemporary movie reviews written between 1999 and the present, *Rotten Tomatoes* synthesises ratings and critical sentiments on a 'tomatometer'. For *They Live*, the tomatometer reads: 'A politically subversive blend of horror and sci-fi, *They Live* is an underrated genre film from John Carpenter.' Moreover, it commands the third-highest percentage in Carpenter's filmography behind *Assault on Precinct 13* (1976) at 97% and *Halloween* (1978) at 94%, almost unheard of numbers on *Rotten Tomatoes* (rarely do films exceed 90%). The few critics of *They Live* knock it for the usual reasons: poor execution, crummy special effects, bad acting, mindless and excessive violence, etc. Most reviewers, however, applaud Carpenter for his capacity for *fusion* – the way he integrates comedy and drama, action and intellect, the old and the new, the cool and the barmy.

They more or less agree that *They Live* is a 'junk movie', but one with style, ingenuity and self-awareness. New, younger audiences who see the film for the first time are generally oblivious to the historical and political context that made it a success. What attracts them to *They Live*, and what makes it a cult phenomenon, is what attracts viewers to professional wrestling, now and in the past: misogyny, violence, absurdity, political incorrectness – and a *jouissance* visible in the execution of these traits that extends from the body of the film to the psyche of the audience.

4

THROUGH A PAIR OF
CHEAP SUNGLASSES DARKLY

SLIDING SOBRIQUETS

On top of being adapted from a story and comic, *They Live* was shaped by input from cast and crew, much like the production of a Shakespearean play, if we agree with critics who claim that Shakespeare did not write his plays himself but in tandem with fellow thespians, playwrights and sideliners, notwithstanding how the bard bootlegged his scripts from older sources. For his part, Carpenter bootlegged the western and situated it in the present day. Steve Swires summarises the writing process:

> Carpenter acquired the film rights to both the short story and the comic-book adaptation. He then wrote a screenplay which combined Nelson's basic story situation with the structure of a classic western, expanding its parameters to accommodate his increasing alarm at the commercialization of popular culture and the insensitivity of political institutions. (1988: 37)

1980s TV had a notable influence on the development of the story. 'I hadn't watched much television over the years, but I began watching TV again', [Carpenter] recounts. 'I quickly realized that *everything* we see is designed to *sell* us something' (quoted in Swires 1988: 37). It is no surprise that actual TVs play a significant role in the film. Ubiquitous and revelatory, they reify the mediatisation and commodification of the body, the self and identity. The imagery and characters we see on TVs in *They Live* purvey its central codes and critiques.

Carpenter's appropriation of 'Frank Armitage', the name credited to the screenwriter, builds upon and calls attention to this layered method of narrative scaffolding and construction. It also endorses the fundamental problem of identity experienced by the protagonist and his human counterparts, who are subliminally automatised by the alien antagonists. Nada lacks a name as well as a home and history; the increasing violence he inflicts throughout the film is as much a bitter revolt against 'nothingness' as an attempt to establish a concrete identity.

Besides this meta-function, Frank Armitage pays homage to H.P. Lovecraft, one of Carpenter's favorite authors.

Like his predecessor 'Martin Quatermass' – the pen name Carpenter assumed on *Prince of Darkness* to honor his debt to British author Nigel (*The Quartermass Xperiment*) Kneale – the selection of 'Frank Armitage' as a pseudonym indicates another influence on Carpenter's career. A character in H.P. Lovecraft's classic story 'The Dunwich Horror', Armitage was a scientist who battled an ancient creature reawakened … 'Lovecraft wrote about the hidden world, the world underneath', Carpenter points out. His stories were about gods who are repressed, who were once on Earth and are now coming back. The world underneath has a great deal to do with *They Live*'. (Swires 1988: 40, 43)

Carpenter's use of the name intimately connects the film with Lovecraft in terms of overlying theme ('the world underneath') and authorship. Lovecraft was a forerunner of 'weird fiction' in the late nineteenth and early twentieth centuries. By contemporary standards, weird fiction of this period is not terribly weird, at least given the dreamlike absurdities, corporeal impossibilities and acausal scenarios we might see in the fiction of Nikolai Gogol, Jorge Luis Borges, Italo Calvino and William S. Burroughs, all of whom wrote narratives that break the laws of genre, convention and representation. Traditional weird fiction predates the niche markets of science fiction, fantasy and horror yet customarily falls into these genres, especially the latter. Lovecraft referred to his literary style as 'cosmicism' or, more broadly, 'cosmic horror'. In these narratives, 'the protagonist comes to realize that he (it is almost always a "he") is a small and puny member of a transient and fragile species poised perilously before natural, supernatural, or extraterrestrial forces that at any time could overwhelm him and all of humanity' (Colavito 2008: 175). Nada, then, is a typical Lovecraftian protagonist.

Making Frank Armitage a character in *They Live* builds another level of signification into the name. Not surprisingly, he is the most complex character, the least 'black-and-white', representing an intricate racial and ideological fissure that impacts the fictional world of the film and the real world of 1980s America. Played by Keith David, Armitage, a former Detroit factory worker, 'befriends' Nada (if we can call it that – they never really like each other) on the construction job Nada finagles when he arrives in Los Angeles. They share the same class, but they possess clear ideological differences. And these differences, the film suggests, are *racially* generated by white bourgeois culture. In an early walk-and-talk dialogue with Nada, Armitage, who must keep a job to support a wife and children back in Michigan, expresses unbridled bitterness

Frank Armitage explains the nature of capitalist reality to Nada.

and enmity for the ruling elite: 'The golden rule: he who has the gold makes the rule. … They close one more factory, we should take a sledge to one of their fancy foreign fuckin' cars. … The whole deal's like some kind of crazy game. They put you at the starting line, and the name of the game is: Make It Through Life. Only everyone's out for themselves and lookin' to do you in at the same time'.

Later, Armitage's dialogue becomes overtly racial. Flustered by Nada's growing suspicions about the Justiceville underground, he says: 'Leave it alone, man. It ain't none of my business. Ain't none of yours. … I got a job now, and I plan on keepin' it. I'm walkin' a white line all the time. I don't bother nobody; nobody bothers me. You better start doin' the same'.

'White line's in the middle of the road', replies Nada gravely. 'That's the worse place to drive.'

Alluding to Frederick Douglass's 1881 essay 'The Color Line' and W.E.B. De Bois's extrapolation of that essay in *The Souls of Black Folk* (1903), the remark indicates sympathy for Armitage and the racial binary that marginalises him. But his initial, pro-capitalist remarks ally him with white bourgeois power, if only psychologically: 'I deliver a hard day's work for money. I just want the chance. It'll come. I believe in America. I follow the rules. Everybody's got their own hard times these days.' The more the film progresses, the further Nada moves away from this sanguine attitude towards the jaded skepticism of Armitage, originally a foil for the protagonist who illuminates his oppositional self. In the end, Nada undergoes an ideological and perceptual overhaul, and he emerges as a *becoming-Armitage*. This transformation corresponds with his *becoming-Piper* and the realisation of the pseudo-psychotic violence enacted by Roddy Piper's wrestling persona. Nada is a kind of template onto which other identities imprint and evolve themselves. In poststructuralist lingo, he is a signifier through which other signifiers (and their connective *signifieds*) slide. Thus Nada as signifier only operates through the medium of other signifiers that use him as a medium (*they live* via Nada, Nada via them). And one of those signifiers, Frank Armitage, is a polyvalent sobriquet. All this verifies a postmodern crisis of identity – in the film, and in general. Identity is not fixed and stable, but unfixed, unstable, capable of change, of construction, destruction and reconstruction. In *They Live*, the chronic vicissitudes of identity both enliven and horrify characters. Likewise do these vicissitudes lead to their freedom, enslavement and death.

ANYPLOT

Combining elements of science fiction and the western, the plot of *They Live* is a conventional masculine brew: stranger comes to town, stranger detects something fishy going on, stranger uncovers the truth, stranger kicks ass and saves the day. Somewhere in the mix is a love interest, usually a *femme fatale* or *femme docile*, almost always a patent sexual object to be ogled and fetishised by the male gaze. We see this recipe literally in *High Plains Drifter* (1973) and metaphorically in *The Matrix* (1999), respective high-grossing western and science fiction genre movies (although the latter also draws heavily on gunslinging tropes). As with much cult cinema, *They Live*'s 'otherness' results from its dumb artifices and its peculiar executions and weird deviations from the formula.

Here's another version of the plot: after losing his job in Denver, Colorado, a penniless itinerant named Nada (who is only named in the credits) goes to LA and finds work in construction. He doesn't have anywhere to sleep and Frank Armitage, a fellow construction worker, takes him to a homeless camp, Justiceville. There is a short period of inactivity and dialogue about social and economic blight. Then Nada begins to notice certain irregularities. A group of vagrants do strange things late at night in a nearby church. Armitage tells him to mind his own business, but Nada won't be derailed. He discovers that Justiceville is a cover for a resistance movement against a race of aliens who have interpolated themselves into everyday life and control human perception and ideology via subliminal messages. Nada goes ballistic and kills several aliens, all of whom the hoodwinked masses think are human. The media christens him a serial killer. He kidnaps a woman, Holly Thompson, the assistant program director at Cable 54 television network. She eludes him. Nada and Armitage have an interminably long conversation during which Nada explains his actions. They join the resistance, but the aliens have been tipped off as to their whereabouts and everybody is blown to shit. Nada and Armitage escape with the knowledge that the device whereby the aliens exert control over humans is a satellite dish on the roof of the Cable 54 skyscraper. They shoot their way to the top. Both characters are killed, but not before taking out the satellite. In the end, the aliens, and the truth, are revealed.

Aside from the implication that the entire world is controlled by one satellite perched atop one building in Los Angeles, this sounds like a fairly standard and 'believable' plot for a science fiction film, one to which blockbuster-tsars Jerry Bruckheimer or Michael Bay might easily administer their prescriptions. Even Peter Nicholls, co-editor of *The Encyclopaedia of Science Fiction*, calls *They Live* an 'excellent formula film' that 'settles for action' (1995: 1218).

But I have left out the good stuff. Which is to say, the bad stuff. Which is to say, the stuff that plugs *They Live* into the outlet of cult cinema.

My rendering of the plot does not account for Nada being played by a professional wrestler distinguished by corny one-liners and awkward, deadwood acting (except when he gets angry and raises his voice, embracing the becoming-Piper, a frequent occurrence). I did not mention that Holly 'eludes' Nada by roundhousing him out of a three-story window, or that Nada and Armitage's 'interminably long conversation' is a seven-and-a-half-minute wrestling match complete with makeshift backbreakers and suplexes, or that the aliens' faces, wax skulls beneath inflated 1980s hairdos, look unspeakably fake and cheesy, or that the aliens possess Dick Tracy wrist-watches, Rolex knockoffs that allow them to communicate with one another and open doorways in the ground, or that the conclusion of *They Live* is punctuated by Nada's middle finger, gratuitous nudity and a raw narrative loose end. Most importantly, I left out the prop on which everything hinges. Without this prop, we might have a very different film.

MONOCHROMATIC ABERRATIONS

The central cult artifice in *They Live* – what facilitates the narrative, impels a hermeneutic of suspicion and contributes to its B-movie caché – are the sunglasses (and later the contact lenses) manufactured by the Justiceville resistance that permit wearers to perceive reality in 'black-and-white', literally and figuratively (or rather, literally by way of a figurative pretence). The naked eye does not perceive reality in black-

and-white, of course. Nor does it view the world in black-and-white through most sunglasses – colour dims or is altered but remains apparent. Carpenter's use of monochrome camerawork to signify the real world as *mis*perceived by the hypnotised masses is an aberration that only really works on a meta-critical, thematic level.

The Wizard of Oz (1939) may be the most widely recognizable cult film in which alterations in colour play a significant role.[20] Use of colour denotes fantasy, the brightly saturated realm of Dorothy's pathological and timeless dreamscape, whereas the blasé rural 1930s dustbowl setting of her reality appears in sepia-toned black-and-white. Colour works as an agential, fabulous and imaginary counterpoint to the 'black-and-white' hardships of poverty, farm life, having your dog confiscated by a mean old lady, and so on. Likewise does colour mark the realm of fantasy in *They Live*, but for a diametrically opposed purpose, delimiting the malignant pathological space constructed by the aliens to maintain human subservience. Black-and-white *mise-en-scènes* represent agency, at least insofar as they represent 'truth', a visual space where subjects perceive reality for what it is, whether they like what they see or not, and whether what they see is 'good' for them or not.

In his creative monograph on *They Live*, Jonathan Lethem writes: 'In *They Live*'s scheme, color is lies, black-and-white the truth. This links the world the … lenses reveal to the *Monolith Monsters*, that black-and-white creature-feature movie seen earlier, and to an era of stripped-down and formally pure cinema Carpenter fears is being overrun by the ethos and aesthetics of the yuppie-Reagan 1980s' (2010: 62). Furthermore, the lenses open a gateway to the past, serving as a (c)ode for Carpenter's beloved black-and-white B-movie sci-fi/horror influences from the 1950s, and etching *They Live* into an unmistakable genealogy of Hollywood cinema. Hence the diegesis availed by and through the lenses exposes *They Live* as a construction, a product of filmmaking by a writer/director (Armitage/Carpenter), just as the reality of the characters therein are constructed and produced by 'writers/directors' (Aliens, products of Armitage/Carpenter). And the characters are constructed on the level of cognition as well as society and culture. Cognitively, their perception is altered and their thoughts are subliminally manipulated. Socially and culturally, they are trained to become ardent capitalist producers and consumers – or to at least desire that subject-position – affecting what they do in private and public spheres, in personal and professional life. The first instance of construction engenders the second, a metaphor for advanced capitalism as it exists in the real, Western world. Media imagery teaches us on a daily basis that consuming merchandise, spending money, increasing debt is 'good' and that any form of economic asceticism or mediation is 'bad'. How we pay for and accumulate and absorb objects engineers ideology and identity.

Robert Cumbow enhances the meta-referential valance of the lenses, identifying a key paradox:

> There are more layers of irony here, however: The black-and-white of *They Live* is not true monochrome, but color film from which the color has been bled in processing. In the objective sequences of the film, what *we* see is also in color, suggesting that our own perception remains deceived even where Nada's and Frank's is not. In a world where seeing … is a synonym for knowing, we're being told that we know nothing. Or at least that we know only what some outside power wants to let us know, which amounts to the same thing. (2000: 172)

This view speaks as much to the characters in *They Live* as it does to late capitalist subjects, who are processed by the clockwork of daily life unaware of the mediatised pathology that (re)produces their minds and bodies, and who are constantly reminded that they 'know nothing' by an always-already growing array of signage and screens.

As with the protagonists of 'Eight O'Clock in the Morning' and 'Nada', 'awakened' characters are subjected to literal signs of the real in *They Live*. The first time Nada sees the world *au naturel* is the first time the audience does. Once again, the lenses of his eyes channel our perception. His 'wake-up call' implicates us as viewers/voyeurs of the filmic diegesis and as subjects of the real-world diegesis (yuppie America) that the film critiques. On the morning after a brutal police raid on Justiceville, Nada's inspection of the ramparts – he is always *inspecting*, vigilant despite his ignorant optimism about 'America' – leads him to the church across the street. Earlier he had snooped around the church and discovered it was not the place of worship and charity that it purported to be. The hymns and instruments of 'choir practice' emanate from a tape recorder and the interior resembles a kind of meth lab, well-used beakers and test tubes scattered across a wooden work table, boxes stacked everywhere, and on a wall, in giant hand-painted letters, the film's ominous thesis: THEY LIVE, WE SLEEP. Nada hears the leaders of the resistance chattering about 'breaking in on top of their signal' and 'send[ing] the shipment out on the street' in the adjacent chapel. After the raid, everything and everyone is gone; the church has been ransacked and cleaned out, the graffiti painted over. Nada finds a leftover box. Fearing detection, he smuggles it into the city and opens it in a deserted alley.

Sunglasses. Ray Bans. The kind Tom Cruise wears in *Risky Business* (1983).[21]

Confused, Nada rifles through the box, but there's nothing else, so he takes a pair, stashes the box in a garbage can to retrieve later, and strolls out of the alley onto a busy street.

He looks like an outsider, even without the 1980s mullet hairdo. The men and women that pass him on the sidewalk wear business suits and dresses. Nada, in contrast, has on his only outfit: denim jeans and a plaid button-down shirt. Immediately, in this commercial urban space, fashion establishes class difference.

He puts on the sunglasses.

He takes them off. This goes on for the next minute or so as Nada struggles with what he sees, comparing the colourful imaginary with black-and-white reality.

In black-and-white reality, images are absent – they only exist in the fictional, mediatised, consumer-capitalist matrix supervised by the aliens. Billboards, road signs, business logos, magazines contain words alone. Formatted in a large, bold-faced, plain font, these words convey the subliminal messages that keep humans at bay. Appropriately, the first word revealed to Nada beneath a billboard advertisement for a computer system sold by 'Control Data' (hint-hint) is: OBEY. The second message he views is less blatant – MARRY AND REPRODUCE – masked by a billboard on which a large-breasted woman in a bikini sunbathes in the ocean surf. Head tossed backwards and shoulders arched, the woman looks virtually orgasmic; a tropical island looms behind her, and scrolled across the blue sky: 'come to the … CARRIBBEAN.' The advertisement and its hidden logos speak to the alpha male gaze and finger humanity as a patriarchal, heterosexual species. The aliens realise that, in order to marry and reproduce, males must take the initiative – thus the lure of the proverbial hot babe.

Nada staggers down the sidewalk and continues to decipher signage. Other messages include: NO INDEPENDENT THOUGHT, CONSUME, CONFORM, SUBMIT, WORK 8 HOURS, SLEEP 8 HOURS, PLAY 8 HOURS and STAY ASLEEP. Then Nada catches a glimpse of an alien skull and

Nada sees the real world in black-and-white.

goes apeshit. To varying degrees and intensities, he continues to go apeshit until the end of the film, manifesting the becoming-Piper.

TELEFISSION

Nada and the audience's view through the sunglasses poses a philosophical dilemma and orchestrates a critique of postmodern culture. In simplest terms, the black-and-white 'word-world' suggests that power belongs to s/he who controls language. Imagery – capitalist imagery, above all, which facilitates the consumption and production of commodities – is an extension of the Word used to pathologise subjects and construct docile bodies; hence image-culture constitutes the realm of subjugation by replicating itself. This basic postmodern tenet reaches a crescendo in the semblance of TV. As Arthur Kroker and David Cook write:

> In postmodernist society, it's not TV as a mirror of society, but just the reverse: *it's society as a mirror of television*. And it's not TV as a reflex commodity-form, but the commodity-form in its most advanced, and exhausted, expression finally … as a pure image-system, as a spectral

television image. ... Television now is the real world of a postmodern culture whose *ideology* is entertainment and the society of the obscene spectacle; whose *culture* is driven onwards by the universalization of the commodity-form ... whose major form of social *cohesion* is provided by the pseudo-solidarities (pseudo-mediations) of electronic television images; whose *public* is the dark, silent mass of viewers who, as Jean Baudrillard says, are never permitted to speak and a media elite which is allowed to speak 'but has nothing to say'. (1986: 268, 269)

Kroker and Cook aptly reference Baudrillard, who theorises the relationship between television and the human condition, making a case for the 'telefission' of 'the real and of the real world; because TV and information in general are a form of catastrophe' (2000: 53). Foremost among such catastrophes are the effects of postmodern implosion, a consequence of image-culture in which illusion becomes indistinguishable from reality and the signs of the real are substituted for the real itself, resulting in hyperreality, the dominion of semantic ruin. For Baudrillard, postmodernity and the twentieth century are defined by 'the immense process of the destruction of meaning' (2000: 160) incited by the fetishisation of capitalist media and *the reification of the self as electronic (and thus immortal) image*.

There is a pertinent example of this idea in *They Live* that occurs at the beginning of the movie, one night before Nada has found a job and settled in to Justiceville. Warming himself by the flames of a bum fire aside other homeless people, he sees somebody watching TV through a window across an alleyway. Onscreen a woman in a red dress discusses her innermost desires with melodramatic delight, caressing her arms as if to prove they exist: 'Sometimes, when I watch TV, I stop being myself and I'm the star of a series, or I have my own talk show, or I'm on the news getting out of a limo and going someplace important. All I ever have to do is be famous. People watch me, and they love me. And I never, never grow old. And I never die.' We don't know who the woman speaks to. Considering the solipsistic tenor of her monologue, she might be speaking to herself. Nada stares on coldly, then sighs and turns his eyes to a helicopter that flutters overhead.

The scene underscores a media pathology that reaches further back than Kroker, Cook and Baudrillard. Affiliates of the Frankfurt School in the first half of the twentieth century posited the human subject as an affectation of the film industry, both as capitalist enterprise and harbinger of image-consciousness. In 'The Work of Art in the Age of Mechanical Reproduction', for instance, Walter Benjamin claims that 'the cult of the movie star, fostered by the money of the film industry, preserves not the unique aura of the person but the "spell of the personality," the phony spell of a commodity' (1969: 231). This very spell binds the woman in red. In another prominent Frankfurt School essay, 'The Culture Industry: Enlightenment as Mass Deception', Max Horkheimer and Theodor Adorno anticipate Baudrillard's concept of implosion by over forty years: 'Real life is becoming indistinguishable from the movies. The sound film, far surpassing the theatre of illusion, leaves no room for imagination or reflection on the part of the audience, who is unable to respond within the structure of the film, yet deviate from its precise detail without losing the thread of the story; hence the film forces its victims to equate it directly with reality' (1972: 126). The onset of television merely accelerated the process, 'victimising' subjects by commodifying and denaturalizing them on a routine and intimate basis.

In these terms, the coloured fantasy world in *They Live* and its corresponding 'negative exposure' critique capitalist image-culture and illustrate a master/slave dialectic. A meta-physical problem arises if we consider the notion that reality is a matter of perception, whether or not the perceived object or space is illusory, simulated or perverted. In this light, the alien image-world is as equally 'real' as the 'real' word-world. And yet technically both worlds are 'unreal', literally construct-ed by the respective technologies of satellites and eyewear, and the latter technology does not present what is seen in its natural form, if only by robbing viewers of colour. No real world, then, exists in the world(s) of *They Live*. 'Meaning' evaporates; the signifier signifies another signifier. Jacked into the matrix of implosion and hyperreality, Nada's anger erupts in part from the telefissure of this central postmodern trauma.

LETHEM ON HOFFMEN

Previously I discussed the complexity of signification Carpen-ter attaches to *They Live* with the name 'Frank Armitage'. He does the same with the 'Hoffman' lenses, as they are called by their makers. What exactly the name references or alludes to is never made clear. There are several possibilities. Lethem divulges three in a chapter entitled 'Assorted Hoffmen':

Some commentators on *They Live* credit 'Hoffman lens-es' as a reference to the accidental discoverer of lyser-gic acid diethylamide, or LSD, the Swiss chemist Albert Hoffmann. This makes an appealingly hip reference to matters of delusion and revelatory insight. ... There's an-other pretty fun candidate: Abbie Hoffman, subversive yippie jester and fugitive, and a paragon of 'us versus them' political stances. ... I'd rather end my report there, but according to the website Realnews247.com, *They Live*'s sunglasses were named in honor of the holocaust denier Michael Hoffman II. Brief lesson for paranoiacs: setting your open-ended conspiracy metaphors loose upon the world, they become (like anything) eligible for manifold repurposing. Free your mind and an ass may follow. (2010: 43)

Every reference point has validity; respective themes of delusion, good vs. evil and revisionist history comprise the narrative centre of *They Live*. Lethem, however, has made a crucial omission: Hoffman was a brand of television set manufactured in the 1950s and 1960s. Moreover, it was among the first TVs to partake in the transition from black-and-white to colour broadcasting and the Tournament of Roses Parade, 'the first prolonged presentation of color video under circumstances where, unlike a studio show, neither lighting nor movement could be controlled' (Gould 1954: 28). Given the pivotal figurative role of TVs in the film, this allusion seems to work most efficiently, punctuating the mediatised pathology/perception suffered by *They Live*'s characters and the late capitalist viewers that watch them. In this instance, television equates directly with the lenses: what we watch corresponds to *what enables us to watch it in a particular ('corrective') way*. The image-oriented panic culture symbolised by the proliferation of TVs has bled onto the subject, onto the cognitive processes by which s/he sees and interprets TV, and the force with which TV *interpellates* the self.

This brings us back to Baudrillard. In *The Ecstasy of Communication*, a treatise on the seductive and zombifying powers of the technological maelstrom, he argues: 'There is no longer any transcendence of depth, but only the immanent surface of operations unfolding, the smooth and functional surface of communication. In the image of television, the most beautiful prototypical object of this new era, the surrounding universe and our very bodies are becoming monitoring screens' (1988:

12). Note that the publication of Baudrillard's text in English falls within the same year of the release of *They Live*. I'm not suggesting that Carpenter was pointing to or even aware of Baudrillard; unlike *They Live*'s prodigal son, *The Matrix*, there are no overt references to him. But the correlation seems obvious considering the anxiety that typified the end of the 1980s. In Baudrillardian lingo, the Hoffman lenses exude this anxiety as symbols for the transformation of subjectivity and the body into objects of *in*fection that have lost their penchant for spectacle and the social and political theatre. The upshot: obscenity. 'We no longer partake in the drama of alienation, but are in the ecstasy of communication. And this ecstasy is obscene. Obscene is that which eliminates the gaze, the image and every representation' (1988: 21–2). By revealing the 'truth', by providing subjects with a 'new' gaze, the Hoffman lenses reify the 'old' gaze, the illusion of telefissional reality, and *the delusion of perception as an individual choice*.

IDEOLOGY AS REAL UNREALITY

When Karl Marx famously calls religion 'the opium of the people', he points to the construction of subjectivity (1978: 54). For Marx, religion imparts a false happiness to subjects who cannot see the real conditions of their pathological capitalist existence. As 'the sigh of the oppressed creature', religion is a profound system of sublimation, a defence mechanism by which life is made liveable. He vies for the abolition of religion, at least as an instrument of corrosive mythmaking, but he appreciates the difficulty of such an exploit, religion being an essential part of capitalist identity. One cannot remove religion without redefining the self.[22]

Over a century later, Guy Debord applied Marx's critique of religion to the 'spectacle', his term for 'society's real unreality'. In all its specific manifestations – news or propaganda, advertising of the actual consumption of entertainment – the spectacle epitomizes the prevailing model of social life' (1967: 13). He even refers to the spectacle as a 'permanent opium war' that 'aims to make people identify goods with commodities and satisfaction with survival that increases according to its own laws' (1967: 30). Here the magnetic, sublimating power of image-culture replaces that of the Christian god; subjects turn their gazes and desires towards electronic media, the cult of celebrity, mindless commodity-consumption and new technologies of misperception, ensuring their continued roles on the stage of Forever.

The *over*world in *They Live*, a 'real unreality', is a spectacular diegesis that operates as a literal and figurative mass opiate. The signal disseminated by the aliens reconfigures human perception *and* psyche; not only does it transform what is seen, it transforms the process of thinking and consequently behaviour in proportion to an explicit capitalist code of ethics. Through chronic hypnosis, the aliens addict humans to capitalist servitude.[23] When the signal is interrupted, humans experience physical withdrawal from the drug of subliminal control as they bear witness to the *under*world. The Hoffman lenses produce the effect. For example, after the first time Nada 'uses' for an extended period and takes the glasses off, he feels fatigued and dizzy. He has just kidnapped Holly and forced her to drive him to her apartment at gunpoint. Slot-eyed, he reclines in the passenger's seat as if poured there, and when they walk inside, he grasps onto Holly's elbow for support. Finally he staggers to a couch and collapses onto the floor. 'It's like a drug', he pants. 'These glasses makes you high, but you come down hard.' Actually the glasses don't produce the high. They remove the effects of a high that has been ingrained into the human sensorium. Like heroin addicts, humans only feel 'normal' when they use the substance that their bodies and minds have been conditioned

Nada comes down hard from the drug-like effects of the Hoffman lenses.

to need. Metaphorically this substance is a 'real unreality', something constructed that feels authentic. Technically it is the electromagnetic waves that fabricate the metaphor.

If people stop using, they experience agitation, headaches, exhaustion, mood swings, and so on. Even the slightest stoppage hurts. Earlier in the film, a character credited only as 'the Drifter' sits beneath the stars with another stock character, 'Family Man', and watches TV – a commercial for press-on nails featuring an attractive blonde woman that noticeably soothes and pleases the Drifter. The face of the resistance ('Bearded Man') interrupts the broadcast. Immediately the viewers become upset, and as Bearded Man explains how 'we are living in an artificially induced state of consciousness', the Drifter barks, 'Goddamn hacker. That's the second time tonight that asshole's cut in!' Wincing, Family Man massages the back of his neck and says, 'This thing's giving me a headache.' 'Yeah, tell me about it,' replies the Drifter, rubbing his temple. 'Must've taken the hackers months to figure out how to do this.' Nada uneasily pinches the bridge of his nose as he walks by and pauses to have a look. Bearded Man's rhetoric is punctuated by bursts of static that consternate the onlookers. At last the Drifter gets up from his tattered armchair and changes the channel, unaware that the source of the interruption comes from across the street in the church. 'Blow it out your ass' he growls with an air of pride, certifying the reinstallation of the mass opiate. On this channel, we see a scene from the slickly referenced pulp sci-fi film *The Monolith Monsters* (1957) – the fleeting image of gigantic spires collapsing and crashing onto two farmhouses. The scene is in black-and-white, whereas the advertisement for press-on nails had been in colour. It foreshadows Nada's imminent awakening via the Hoffman lenses, which destroy his formerly optimistic and innocent conception of reality and America.

In addition to its psychosomatic impact, the alien's signal has a resonant theoretical component. Specifically, the signal – its deployment, its effects – makes a statement about ideology.

> The theme of *They Live* … is the necessity to see through the obfuscating haze of dominant ideology. In the story, aliens have infiltrated human society and control the media, literally creating what Frankfurt School theorists would call its 'false consciousness' encoded in television signals that create, according to a subversive hacker, 'an artificially induced state of consciousness that resembles sleep'. People must wear special sunglasses to become aware of the subtextual messages of the media that exhort us to be happy, reproduce and consume. The film offers an Althusserian critique of the mass media as Ideological State Apparatus ('they live; we sleep'), and the aliens are monstrous only insofar as we recognize them as smart capitalists – they are, as one human collaborator explains, free enterprisers for whom the Earth is 'just another developing planet. We're their Third World'. (Grant 2004: 16)

Louis Althusser developed his concept of the Ideological

State Apparatus (ISA) in a seminal essay first published in 1970, 'Ideology and Ideological State Apparatuses: Notes towards an Investigation' (2008). Influenced by Marx and Jacques Lacan, he argues that ISAs (social institutions like the church, family, media, schools and government) subjectify individuals through a process called interpellation, binding them materially and psychologically to ISAs whether they like it or not, since the effects of ISAs cannot be extracted from daily life. We are always-already interpellated by ideology. And yet ideology is an 'illusion/allusion', a 'representation of the imaginary relationship of individuals to their real conditions of existence' (2008: 36). In other words, ideology distorts how we think about ourselves and the cultural forces that produce us. It appears natural and organic. But ideology is a construct that only alludes to the real; therefore ideology, like Debord's spectacle, is a 'real unreality', a fantasy that ready-made subjects collectively misinterpret. We can't escape from ideology either – it has no 'outside', as the outside is the inside, and vice versa. 'One of the effects of ideology is the practical *den-egation* of the ideological character of ideology by ideology: ideology never says, "I am ideological"' (2008: 49). To do so would necessitate a subject-position outside of the system, an impossibility.

They Live illuminates several ISAs, but the dominant ISA belongs to capitalist media, the vehicle whereby the aliens 'live' and humans 'sleep'. When humans perceive the subliminal messages through Hoffman lenses, they also perceive the ISA that interpellates them. Not literally, of course – one cannot see a system of beliefs. Rather, the Hoffman lenses spark an epistemological awakening, creating an awareness of the powers that have used ideology as a means of control, submission and surveillance. Most of all, they draw attention to class, the foremost architect of identity and perception in both the film and Althusser's theory. 'Whatever their form (religious, ethical, legal, political), [ISAs] always express *class positions*' (2008: 33).

Althusser conceptualises ideology as imaginary and subjectifying. He further claims that 'ideology has no history' (ibid.), connecting it with Freud's definition of the unconscious as eternal. 'If eternal means, not transcendent to all (temporal) history, but omnipresent, trans-historical and therefore immutable in form throughout the extent of history, I shall adopt Freud's expression word for word, and write *ideology is eternal*, exactly like the unconscious' (2008: 35). In *They Live*, this idea manifests in the dominant ISA, which lacks an origin: nobody knows when the aliens first abducted and inscribed human perception, bodies, culture, ideology. For that matter, nobody knows where the aliens came from. Once the truth is uncovered, Armitage asks Nada: 'How long have they been there?' 'Who knows,' Nada replies. 'What are they? Where did they come from?' 'Well, they ain't from Cleveland.' Nada's jibe enrages Armitage, but he soon concludes: 'Maybe they've always been with us, those things out there.'

If only for lack of knowledge and history, the aliens signify ideology as ubiquitous and eternal – as the 'outside' (i.e. the 'inside'). Armitage and Nada confirm this problem when they infiltrate the alien underground and witness their method of transport: cosmic teleportation. Ushered through the underground by the Drifter, who has become an alien friendly and abandoned his Justiceville rags for a snazzy tux, the estranged duo watch two figures in business suits step onto a portal, one at a time. Carrying luggage, they demolecularise and beam into deep space as pulsing points of light. 'I don't know how it works exactly,' the Drifter says, 'but it has to do with some sort of gravitational lens deal, bending the light or some damn thing. But you can move from place to place, world to world if you want to. You see, the whole thing, it works like one big airport.'

A bourgeois alien prepares for cosmic flight.

Nada and Armitage stare on in disbelief. But they (and we) only learn how the aliens move – not where they come from, or how long they have been on Earth. The Drifter doesn't care as long as he can profit from them. The moral turpitude that so deeply affects and provokes Nada has no influence on the upwardly mobile Drifter, who, as a sell-out to the aliens (and thus the capitalist system), exclusively equates identity with economy, despite being enslaved. 'Boys, lemme tell ya,' he declares, 'they got their act together – believe you me.' This vote of confidence, and the Drifter's contented and proud tone, correlates with how many Southern American slaves perceived their masters. Slaves were robbed of an identity – legally, socially, fiscally, psychologically – and often lived vicariously through their masters, fighting over whose master best had his 'act together'. The Drifter's position is not far from this manner of thinking. That he talks in a good-old-boy Southern drawl underlines the correlation.

Althusserian theory, as with all forms of theory, can be applied to any text, in any medium. I want to make the argument that cult films are exceptionally ripe for theorisation in light of the hyperbolic ways they often parody, satirise, politicise or simply represent themes that cultural critics engage – namely class, gender and race. By absence or emphasis, these themes come to bear in most contemporary narratives, whatever their form. *They Live* italicises and exaggerates all of them.

Carpenter openly foregrounds the issue of class, but we also see racial and gender treatments through the development of relationships between Nada and Armitage and Nada and Holly. Moreover, the characters are marked as racial and gendered bodies by discourse as much as by action and reaction. Nada's precarious one-liners expose his subjectivity. Recall his claim that 'life's a bitch – and she's back in heat,' a masculinised critique that first projects the demon of femininity onto the entire ontological sphere, and then animalises femininity (and ontology), likening it to the wiles of a mad dog. By this logic, the aliens pose a threat to (white) masculinity, and the threat activates Nada as Becoming-Piper. We might also say that racial and class tensions in the film are an effect of the same problem; they occur because masculinity is put in jeopardy, and they are exacerbated because male subjects fight to regain masculinity.

Nada – his words, his actions, his image and his meta-textual resonance – represents the phallic core of this gendered reading. And it is through his phallic core that viewers perceive the world of *They Live*. Nada appears in nearly every scene, and with a few exceptions (e.g. Armitage putting on the sunglasses for the first time), we see things through his eyes. We experience the latter stages of the production of Nada as a gendered capitalist subject. But what are the roots of his production? What are the traumatic kernels that contributed to his adulteration? To find the answer, we must turn to another important ISA: the family. The way *They Live* depicts the family suggests that we may be viewing the wish-fulfilment fantasy of a pathological subject who attempts to fill a dire lack – a scenario reflecting upon the psychological condition of Nada *and* the audience.

5

THE PATHOLOGICAL UNCONSCIOUS

PARENTAL GUIDANCE AND THE AMERICAN NIGHTMARE

Nada's upbringing reveals a lot about his character. And yet his upbringing is hardly revealed. Still he is not, as his name would have him, 'nobody'. He has a history that acutely informs the flows of his desires.

There is only one reference to a mother figure in a wisecrack uttered during Nada's first killing spree. Levelling a shotgun at an alien yuppie reporting him into a wristwatch radio transmitter, he says: 'Mama don't like tattle-tales.' This might seem insignificant. Certainly it's a goofy thing to say. And that's the point: protagonists cast in the mould of Hollywood action heroes, even in cult films, are nothing without their banal witticisms. But the remark seems more evocative than others, suggesting that Nada's mother, or mothers in general, are scornful of certain behaviour. Here we have a negative portrayal of the mother figure. And, again, the *only* portrayal. Maternal lack defines a key coordinate of Nada's parental triangulation. The lack makes sense. It is also necessary. Violent and hypermasculine, Nada is the product of an abusive father. In the broader spectrum, he is a symptom of an oppressive (and repressing) patriarchy.

For Nada, the father figure takes three forms, all of which fail him. First: his actual parent. Second: the aliens. Finally, by extension: America itself.

Doggo with Armitage, Nada drinks beer and reminisces about the cruelty of his father:

A long time ago, things were different. My old daddy, he took me down to the river, kicked my ass, told me about the power and the glory. I was saved. He changed when I was little. Turned mean. Started tearing at me. So I ran away when I was thirteen. Tried to cut me once. Big old razor blade. Held it up against my throat. I said, 'Daddy, please.' It just kept moving back and forth, like he was sawing down a little tree.

Nada's backstory leads Armitage to associate his father with the aliens, wondering if they are mere sadists who thrive on 'seeing us hate each other, watching us kill each other off, feeding on our own cold fuckin' hearts'. His face a mask of stone, Nada replies, 'Well I got news for 'em. There's gonna be hell to pay. Cuz I ain't daddy's little boy no more.'

His father remains elusive. Did he baptise Nada in the river, and was he a preacher? Or is this image a metaphor for his character? What kind of metaphor? What made him change into an ostensible sadist? Why did he 'kick his ass' before the change? Whatever the answers to these questions, the point is clear: Daddy traumatised Nada, physically and psychologically, forcing him to make his own way from a young age in a patriarchal, dog-eat-dog world. Nada emerges as the symbolic residue of a familial lack. What little parental guidance he

In the worst possible taste, Piper blindsides Fijian wrestler Jimmy 'Superfly' Snuka on an episode of 'Piper's Pit', nailing him on the head with a coconut.

received, if only mnemonically, was negative and violent. Here is another reason why 'Rowdy' Roddy Piper serves Carpenter so well in this role; his violent history as a professional wrestler – familiar to most viewers in the late 1980s – immediately informs the character.[24] Even before *They Live*'s central conflict gains momentum, Nada-Piper seems on the edge, like a viper, always about to strike or explode, just as he did on scores of occasions in 'Piper's Pit', luring his guests into thinking he was their friend, and then, when they let down their guard, blindsiding them, pulverizing them – *injecting the venom*. As a result, his screen presence instils a constant anxiety in viewers, from the moment we see him walking the streets at the beginning of the film to his last rebellious breaths at the end.

'I ain't daddy's little boy no more' – the thesis of Nada's backstory is paradoxical. In fact, Nada *is* his father's little boy. Shaped by a malicious violence and subsequent absence, he always will be. In Lacanian discourse, Nada's symbolic identification with an ego-ideal and the phallic order is established on cruel and volatile grounds that terminally extend into his adult life. He may have escaped his real father. But he cannot escape the symbolic father. In *They Live*, Daddy reappears in the form of the aliens, who themselves come to represent the evils of American capitalism. This return of the repressed capsizes Nada's formerly optimistic view of America as a productive, virtuous society. He trusts America, just as he trusted his father, who 'saved' him. Then, taking his father's lead, America 'turned mean' and 'started tearing at [him]'. The aliens become the throbbing symptom of this recurrence. Revealing a proverbial smiling veneer and gruesome underbelly, literally and figuratively, they symbolise the promise of a fair shot – the idea that, in America, even the proles on skid row can prevail and flourish, when all along they have been kicking Nada while he's down.

The aliens can be read as tell-tales for the American Dream, which, as a seminal tool of American capitalism, ordinarily asserts the prospect of widespread social and economic escalation, but culminates in virtual stagnation.

The American Dream always involves class and capital. It does not always involve climbing the social ladder or acquiring capital. As we see in, say, Beat literature of the 1950s, the American Dream derives from a rejection of capitalist mores and modes of conduct in favour of an anti-conformist, gleefully disenfranchised Bohemianism. In cinema, *Easy Rider* (1969) exemplifies a Beat lifestyle and ideology, which contributes to its cult status. Likewise with *They Live*, even if Nada, in contrast to the protagonists of *Easy Rider*, regards the American Dream in pro-capitalist terms, so to speak, given his reaction when he realises the Dream is just that – a dream. Or, more accurately, a nightmare.

In every context, the American Dream belongs to the realm of desire and the formative experiences that construct the flows of desire. It is a subjective experience … and loss.

While large demographics (of labourers, homeless people, etc.) can intimately relate to his plight, the quest for the American Dream that unfolds in the film is Nada's quest, especially if we consider the role of his traumatic history and the many ways in which *They Live* is shot from Nada's perspective visually, emotionally and psychologically. This suggests that what we watch might be a pathological wish-fulfilment fantasy. Nada's father revisits him in the guise of alien yuppies intent on 'saw[ing] him down', and by revolting against and exposing his antagonists for what they are, he avenges himself, symbolically defeating the real father who he ran away from as a child, their 'differences' unresolved. He fills the lack that defines his subject-position. As a result, he accomplishes a kind of therapeutic closure. But only at the price of his life. Lack is the playground of desire, and desire cannot be killed as long as the mind-body apparatus that houses it remains alive. There is no escape. Nada 'wins' and the fantasy comes to a close. And the ghost of his father ushers him into the grave.

Nada's interpellation by the familial ISA avows 'the growing stress on the American family and its proper child-rearing functions' that gained momentum in the 1980s and reached a climax in the year of *They Live*'s release (see Boozer 2007: 168). Studying the 1988 films *Fatal Attraction*, *Three Men and a Baby*, *Baby Boom* and *Raising Arizona*, all concerned with 'the stressed family and "adoptive" parenting', Jack Boozer discusses the 'rapidly changing status of the American family, which was no longer the assumed two-parent-and-children nuclear norm with the mother at home for the rearing of children' (2007: 184). Much of this shift had to do with the close of the Reagan era.

This age of rapacious high rollers, government deregulation, runaway covert activities, bloated military spending, and a leisure world with cocaine as the glamorous drug of choice was well represented and critiqued in these films. So too were the concerns about the growing dependence on commercial television for one's view of the world, and the increasing vulnerability of the nuclear family to all of these and other challenges. ... The long era of 'avarice as state religion' had become weighed down with economic and social debt by the end of the year, and most of the Hollywood films cited here seemed to be sounding some version of a wake-up call. (Ibid.)

Not coincidently does Carpenter refer to *They Live* as an explicit 'wake-up call'. Although quite different than the mainstream films Boozer talks about, *They Live* has the same concerns with the condition of America during this period – none more, perhaps, than 'avarice as state religion' and its effects on the nuclear family, the individual and American identity in general. Nada is a symptom of this pathological order. The prodigal son of multiple violent father figures – including, now, Ronald Reagan himself – he reacts to the forces of oppression with a graphic execution of the very masculinity that authorises them, amping up the machismo as he struggles to even the score.

MACHO MYTHS

In its inner, upper ranks and on the screens that constitute its body, the Hollywood culture industry has always been ordained by the laws of patriarchy. Mainstream films are made by males, for males. And the male gaze dictates the narrative of celluloid dreams. Masculinity as normative, femininity as pathological – despite exceptions like the feminist filmmaking movement,[25] this binary is a historic cinematic staple. It prevails in the twenty-first century more than ever in the heat of the economic recessions of the 2000s and 2010s and the increasing degree to which moviemaking unreservedly depends upon capital. Even indie film companies, regardless of their apparent proliferation since the 1990s, have been consistently threatened, hedged and assimilated by Conglomerate Hollywood to the extent that, what might seem indie (by brand and by content) is would-be blockbuster in disguise.[26]

In her influential feminist essay, 'Visual Pleasure and Narrative Cinema', Laura Mulvey uses psychoanalysis to explore the phallocentric 'fascination of film', which is 'reinforced by pre-existing patterns of fascination already at work within the individual subject and the social formations that have moulded him. … Film reflects, reveals and even plays on the straight, socially established interpretation of sexual difference which controls images, erotic ways of looking and spectacle' (2001: 393). As for popular American cinema, she states: 'The magic of the Hollywood style at its best (and of all the cinema which fell within its sphere of influence) arose, not exclusively, but in one important aspect, from its skilled and satisfying manipulation of visual pleasure. Unchallenged, mainstream film coded the erotic into the language of the dominant patriarchal order' (2001: 395). Hollywood cinema – the way is it constructed and how we are constructed to perceive it – is always-already inscribed by a masculine ethos, ideology and system of values. Capitalist mathematics: this is what sells; hence this is what exists.

By its very transgressive nature, cult cinema undermines the authority and authorship of phallocentrism. Consider *The Rocky Horror Picture Show* (1975), *The Toxic Avenger* (1984) and *Sin City* (2005), all of which problematise and parody gender roles in uniquely self-conscious ways, but primarily by way of hyperbole, exaggerating masculinity and femininity to a point of mutant excess, literally and metaphorically.[27] These films, however, are still by and about male subjectivity, if only as a critique of patriarchy in the Hollywood culture industry and in the wider American cultural sphere that bore and inscribed them.

They Live falls into the same 'camp'. We see mutant excess in the zombified bodies and capitalist practices of the aliens alongside the evolving (and reactive) alpha-maleness of Nada as Becoming-Piper. These excesses reaffirm Carpenter's socioeconomic critique of 1980s excess, and Nada's hyper-masculinity allies *They Live* with mainstream action cinema *à la* Schwarzenegger, Stallone and other anabolic/phallic bodies. More specifically, Nada's hypermasculinity reasserts the notion that the film is a pathological wish-fulfilment fantasy conjured to fill a traumatic lack. This rings true more and more as the narrative progresses and turns from leftist analysis to unadulterated action. '*They Live* … abandons its cultural critique halfway through to concentrate on the improbable heroics of its solitary hero Nada. … Ironically, the film becomes exactly the kind of formulaic escapist entertainment it begins by critiquing as the opiate of the people, when Nada single-handedly destroys the alien's sole (!) broadcasting station, apparently saving the world' (Grant 2004: 18).

The multiplication of improbabilities such as a sole broadcasting station – and its destruction by Nada himself, saving the world in the tradition of countless action-heroes before him – lend themselves to the idea that he has experienced a schizophrenic breakdown, a condition that extends vicariously to the film's viewership and the capitalist matrix that contains and codes that viewership. I will use the language of schizoanalysis to articulate this idea. Deleuze has argued that 'schizophrenia is indissociable from the capitalist system, itself conceived as primary leakage (*fuite*): an exclusive malady' (1995: 72). Together with Félix Guattari in *Anti-Oedipus* (1972) and *A Thousand Plateaus* (1980), he develops a theory of technologised desire in which subjects are forced to negotiate the mad, deterritorialising tentacles of capitalism, a process that itself involves an act of madness, of psychic arbitration.

> There is a twofold movement of decoding or deterritorializing flows on the one hand, and their violent and artificial reterritorialization on the other. The more the capitalist machine deterritorializes, decoding and axiomatizing flows

in order to extract surplus value from them, the more its ancillary apparatuses, such as government bureaucracies and the forces of law and order, do their utmost to re-territorialize, absorbing in the process a larger and larger share of surplus value. (Deleuze & Guattari 1998: 34–5)

Acts of reterritorialisation are not limited to an ISA; individual subjects perform them, too. 'The schizophrenic deliberately seeks out the very limit of capitalism: he is its inherent tendency brought to fulfilment, its surplus product, its proletariat, and its exterminating angel. He scrambles all the codes and is the transmitter of the decoded flows of desire' (1998: 35). Nada is a perfect candidate to theorise within this rubric, both as a Deleuzoguattarian schizo and as an actual, clinical schizo, one who has suffered an implosion of reality and fantasy, or rather, one whose reality has been usurped by a compensatory fantasy. *They Live* becomes a symptom of Nada's illness. And his illness signifies a larger cultural pathology that 1980s audiences could empathise with.

Theorised or not, Nada's actions and reactions, the things he does and what he says, are decidedly masculine, violent and chauvinistic – *macho* through and through. But does *They Live* endorse or critique this conduct? Ken Jurkiewicz wonders about Carpenter's intentions: 'Isn't the kind of macho-male bonding and rugged individualism once again celebrated in this film exactly the kind of counterproductive *mythmaking* that keep us sedated and asleep? Isn't Carpenter's left-wing message radically subverted by the very genre that he has chosen to utilize?' (1990: 38).

The gratuitous shot of a woman's breasts at the end of the film, a final symbolic orgasm led up to by Nada's macho-male heroics, may substantiate Jurkiewicz's inference: *They Live* uses liberal politics as a front for its real purpose to provide eye candy for the male gaze. Thus Carpenter reinforces rather

A final symbolic orgasm.

than subverts the myths of gender construction that its genre predecessors wore like a badge. This line of thought has validity, but it is too simplistic and reductive given the meta-narrational complexity of *They Live*. The film's use of hyperbole alone signals a critique of itself as a genre production, taking obscene pleasure in its own exaggerated antics. This is true whether we are talking about larger issues like gender performativity or minor details like blocking techniques. Consider Nada himself. We know that's not Nada. That's *Piper*. Rowdy Roddy Piper. At no point would 1980s viewers think otherwise, partly because of bad acting – we never lose ourselves in his performance – but mostly because we know him as a professional wrestler with a big mouth and a bad temper. From the first time we see Nada sombrely walking the streets of Los Angeles, we see Piper, and we know that it's only a matter of time before he explodes into himself.

EITHER PUT ON THESE GLASSES, OR START EATIN' THAT TRASH CAN: PART 1

They Live's hypermasculine motif reaches a crescendo – a very lo-o-o-ong crescendo – during the infamous fight scene between Nada and Frank Armitage. Many critics and reviewers have argued that the scene is disposable: cut it from the spool and nothing would be lost. On the contrary, the film's major themes of race, gender, sexuality and violence converge at this coordinate of stupid(ly) prolonged aggression. Furthermore, the scene stems from an extensive tradition of mano-a-mano brawls in cinema that Carpenter aspired to outdo. The result is *They Live* at its most hyperbolic.

Nada and Armitage's physical clash reflects Carpenter's own creative clash with cinematic history and films that inspired him but that he wanted to *beat*. In an interview with Gilles Boulenger, Carpenter references John Ford's *The Quiet Man* (1952), which culminates in a stop-and-start, get-up-and-get-knocked-down punchfest between Sean Thorton (John Wayne) and Will Danaher (Victor McLaglen), who are followed by a horde of excited villagers as they blunder through the streets of Innisfree, a fictional Irish town: 'The fight sequence in *The Quiet Man* isn't that good. In my mind, it was better than it is in reality. It's very quick. There's nothing much to it' (Boulenger 2003: 212). Carpenter is a bit hard on *The Quiet Man*, made over thirty years before *They Live* for an audience with different cinematic expectations and experiences. In its time, the scene was a great success and a fitting climax to the romantic drama, which won Academy Awards for best director and cinematography. More curious is Carpenter's concern that Ford's fight wasn't realistic, but 'better' than realistic, a hyperreal exchange of blows that could only exist on celluloid. In *They Live*, he wanted something grittier and more believable. Ironically, what we get is something that stretches and in some instances tears the fabric of reality.

In the same interview, Boulenger asks Carpenter why he made the fight so long, contending that it 'becomes purely gratuitous from a narrative point of view', the most telling sign of its digression from realism. Carpenter responds:

First, I wanted to do a great long fight. Secondly, I had actors who were physically capable of that kind of fight. Roddy worked with Keith David for a month and a half on that fight to the point where they were making contact. It wasn't the old-fashion western hit. They really went right at it, and that was what made the fight as convincing as it was. What made the sequence work also is that we used a Panaglide camera to follow them around. So the scene is more like a ballet. (2003: 212)

A 'stabilizing device worn by the camera operator', the Panaglide was an early version of the Steadicam, which 'permits fluid camera movement, allows greater mobility than tracking shots, and minimizes shakiness' (Pramaggiore & Wallis 2008: 149). Carpenter had used this technology before in *Halloween* for the POV of Michael Myers, 'most famously in the virtuoso opening subjective sequence, which gives the appearance of being a single shot, though there are several disguised cuts' (Hall 2004: 73). He does not use the Panaglide in *They Live* to convey a single shot; the fight contains numerous cuts, none of them rough, and the camera maintains a balanced position, seeming to move on ball bearings. The goal is to depict a greater sense of realism with smooth camerawork and draw less attention to the medium whereby viewers are able to see into the film world. But the effect belies realism, as Carpenter admits: 'the scene is more like a ballet' than a real fight. Again we fall into hyperreality. Nada and Armitage are hardly suited for a staging of *The Nutcracker*; they 'dance' like barbarians, not ballerinas. In terms of how we *see* them move, the scene is too real, or more real than real, made such by the very smooth camerawork that intends to conceal itself. For all of its hard knocks, cinematic presentation renders the fight a mock-fight more akin to what we would encounter in the diegesis of professional wrestling, and Nada and Armit-

age become proverbial duelling Chaunticleers. Which is precisely the rub. Notwithstanding Carpenter's desire to surpass
predecessors like John Ford, his fight emerges more from a
love of wrestling than anything else. As Jurkiewicz recounts:

> Indeed, in a sequence which seems more like a tribute
> to Roddy Piper's once-and-future employers, the World
> Wrestling Federation, than it is a standard action-movie
> setpiece, Nada must literally beat the almost terminally
> stubborn Frank into initially putting on his pair of Hoffman
> lenses; the film insists that people will vehemently re-
> sist seeing the truth about the futile nature of their lives.
> (1990: 38)

Chronic disavowal as a necessary, if not definitive, element of
the human condition – fair enough. But Armitage's resistance
transcends mere obstinacy.

The fight takes place in the alley where Nada stashed the
box of Hoffman lenses. When he comes back to get them,
the box is gone, collected by a garbage truck just moments
ago. Nada sneaks up behind the truck, opens the trunk and
climbs in, furiously searching. He finds the box … and the truck
driver, unaware that the trunk is ajar, rotates the compactor
and accidentally dumps Nada out on a surging bed of rubbish,
then drives away. Centre-screen, with the camera at a slight
up-angle, Nada stands, almost triumphantly, gripping the box
and a pair of sunglasses. As a human (subjugated by evil alien
masters) and lower-class citizen (supervised by bourgeois alien
capitalists), Nada is detritus, residual and disposable – a hang-
nail on the finger of the (capitalist) social body. Here he literally
adopts that subject-position. And yet, for a moment, he looms
tall above the waste, resolute, like a lord of flies.

Unknown to Nada, Armitage followed him. 'Yo,' he gripes,
perturbed, standing next to a dumpster. 'One week's pay. It's

Lord of the Flies.

the best I could do.' He tosses a wad of cash at Nada, who quickly puts on the sunglasses to ensure Armitage's humanity, then implores him to try on the sunglasses, striding forward … Armitage punches him in the nose, hard. Stunned, Nada wipes blood from his nostrils with his wrist, examines the blood, and delivers a cold, hard stare – a familiar gaze delivered to many opponents in the wrestling ring. We sense the imminent transition from Jekyll-Nada into Hyde-Piper. 'I'm trying to save you and your family's life,' he explains. Enraged, Armitage yells, 'You couldn't even save your own!' Nada punches him on the nose now, harder, spinning him around and knocking him down, face-first into the dumpster.

'I'm giving you a choice,' Nada huffs. 'Either put on these glasses, or start eatin' that trash can!' 'Not this year', Armitage retorts. And the barbaric ballet commences.

It's not terribly strange that Armitage and Nada strike one another with such force; resentment and angst has been building between them since they met. But the freakish brutality exerted during the next five minutes falls into the realm of irrealism, possessing an absurdist, almost dreamlike quality. Normal modes of causality don't add up. One moment Nada pleads with Armitage to do as he says, the next he's raining blows on him like a homicidal maniac, or like a hyperactive child who can't get his way. Piper often behaved this way in the ring and in interviews, distracting his opponent/ interlocutor with 'soft words', or feigning an injury, and then unleashing the inner beast.

After the first exchange of blows, Nada reluctantly says, 'I don't wanna fight ya,' but Armitage, pissed off, swings wildly, and Nada repeats, 'I don't wanna fight ya,' deflecting jabs. 'Stop it!' Nada commands. 'No!' Armitage cries. So Nada pegs him with a right hook that would take off most people's heads. This kind of behaviour escalates as the fight goes on, Nada attacking Armitage with a two-by-four at one point (seconds later he apologises, laughs even). Fighting in a movie almost always differs from fighting in the real world, even if a movie endeavours to capture 'realism', which does not mean capturing how long a real fight might last and how capable and skilful fighters are, but how the physical body responds to trauma. Most cinematic mêlées – especially of the Kung Fu variety – would be over in seconds. Audiences know this and suspend disbelief accordingly. *They Live*'s mêlée is far from, say, the fantastical, high-tech *wuxia pian* of *The Matrix*, but it's still markedly weird, even by cinematic standards of adaptive/extrapolative realism.

Weirdest of all is the sheer length of the fight. The longer it goes on – stopping, threatening to end, then starting again – the stranger (and more estranging) it becomes, defying normative timeframes of cinematic violence. As I watched it for the first time in the theatre, I vividly remember my evolving disbelief amid the groans and guffaws of the audience reacting to what they likely perceived as either silliness or daring on the part of the filmmaker. By the time the fight was over, Armitage beaten to a point that he couldn't stop Nada from shoving the sunglasses onto his face, it seemed like thirty minutes had passed. Intentions and effects aside, Carpenter had certainly shot a 'great long fight'.

The fight's *moves* complement its absurd length. Nada and Armitage don't just punch each other. They execute an assortment of wrestling techniques, including choke holds, body drops, head butts, eye gouges, and my favourite, an all-out crotch attack during which Armitage crawls atop Nada and rams his knee into Nada's groin five times (cast in silhouette, they might be mistaken for two men having rough sex). This is no street fight. It's a taste of Wrestlemania that happens to erupt on the street. As such, it's *disruptive*. The fight sticks out like a sore thumb and jars us awake, as it were, because it breaks the ontological laws that the rest of the film obeys. Piper consumes Nada here; we know it, and we revel in it. But the effect remains uncanny. And this is why the fight is 'great' – in and of itself and as a cult artefact. The fight 'succeeds' because it fails to achieve realism even as viewers suspend their disbelief. It's great because it's idiotic and bangs the gongs of *jouissance*.

After the fight, Piper retreats into Nada like a poltergeist, temporarily exhausted by and exorcised of his powers. We know he'll be back, stronger and madder, spitting venom and pulverizing aliens, for a climax that promises more than it could possibly deliver. At this point, *They Live* casts itself as a metafiction more than anywhere else, illuminating the constructed, formulaic, pieced-together contours of the cinematic body. Nada has been denaturalised and, like the world he lives in, exposed as a hoax, or at least a façade. And Piper is a façade – not a person, but a persona, forged by the pop universe of professional wrestling. Likewise with the medium that interpellates Nada-Piper. By rupturing diegetic reality and calling attention to its own clockwork, *They Live* critiques the production of cinema itself, principally the action-hero blockbusters it borrows from and artfully drags through the gutters.

Finally, the irreality of the fight scene points to the idea that the film may be a pathological, would-be agential fantasy

Nada-Piper administers a makeshift suplex on his opponent.

playing out on Nada's mindscreen. From this angle, *They Live* foregrounds one man's subjective and unconscious desires over the emanations of society and culture at large. By 'one man', I mean Nada ... but I also mean *Carpenter*. As John Muir notes, the fight is about the film's director more than the protagonist and the film itself:

This strange fight comes from Carpenter's love of professional wrestling, and the battle indeed comes across like a WWF event. The characters lift and throw each other, but they are not on a cushioned mat – they are on hard asphalt streets! This fact throws believability out the window in a way the aliens, conspiracies and gunfight never could. Indeed, this fight sequence seems to confirm the alien point of view that human beings are stupid animals. The obvious truth about this fight scene is that there is no real dramatically motivated reason for Frank and Nada to fight one another. Yet, to give the devil his due, this fight is pure Carpenter: brilliantly staged, shot and edited. And it again demonstrates Carpenter's total individuality as a filmmaker. He included this fight because he enjoyed it – audience and dramatic needs be damned! A viewer might prefer the more elegant style of fighting demonstrated in *Big Trouble in Little China*, but at the time of *They Live*, Carpenter wanted to explore the use of professional wrestling in film – and *They Live*, like all of Carpenter's films, clearly is a product of its director's personal vision. (2000: 150)

EITHER PUT ON THESE GLASSES, OR START EATIN' THAT TRASH CAN: PART 2

So far I have focused on the effects, and the affectedness, of the fight scene as a meta-narrational anomaly and superfluity. In his monograph, Jonathan Lethem explores some of the fight's broader thematic subtexts and the relationship between Nada and Armitage. Most compelling are his insights on homoeroticism and race relations. In a chapter entitled 'Gay Porn', Lethem describes Nada and Armitage's first exchange as a kind of 'winky-nudgy' overture: 'Nada's black, construction-worker colleague … sidles up to the topless hero, then arches his eyebrow and purrs: "You need a place to stay? Justiceville's over on Fourth Street. They got food and showers. I'm goin' there if you want me to show you"' (2010: 34). What distinguishes the exchange as a prelude to a porn film, Lethem argues, has to do with body image, body language, enunciation, intertextuality and the medium itself.

Partly it's the fluffy excess of Roddy Piper's musculature, so smooth and top-heavy, so unlike that of the actors and extras he's surrounded by, so unlike a real construction worker. Partly it's the sweet-beneath-the-gruffness gift of Keith David's expressive face, and the burnished and insinuating Barry White quality of his vocal delivery. But even more, it may be that the low-budget vagueness of the movie up to this point is *already* reminiscent of a porn film, specifically of pornography's typical interval of stalling before getting down to its horny business. If we've even half-consciously registered some uneasiness about the film's purposes, we might now be tempted to think that maybe it was that kind of business, now underway at last. (2010: 34–5)

The first half of the film, then, constitutes an interval of stalling – from the point of Armitage and Nada's introduction to the first punches of the fight scene … which we might call the first kisses of the fuck scene. Desire defers until this symbolic act of sex that plays out as an act of violence. As in the illustration of Armitage's crotch attack, sometimes the violence looks like sex. It is more intimately connected to the narrative constitution of porn sex: both the fight/fuck scene and pornographic films involve elements of the corny (absurd dialogue, goofy preliminary scenarios, clumsy blocking techniques) and the hardcore (explicit sex and/or graphic violence). Sex and violence chronically interrelate in *They Live*, not only between Armitage and Nada, but between Nada and Holly. The latter couple never have sex. They exude sexual tension, though, and their relationship begins, develops and ends in turbulent waters.[28] But the real love relationship belongs to Nada and Armitage.

Earlier I suggested that depictions of hypermasculinity in 1980s American media served to compensate for Cold War terror and paranoia. In the case of Nada and Armitage, excessive masculinity also serves as a deflection (or *in*flection) of repressed homosexual desire. Their fighting/fucking signifies the crux of a primal Freudian dynamic linking aggression with sexuality. If we think of it as a representation of broader cultural conflict, the 1980s might be characterised by a widespread fear of apocalyptic mushroom clouds as much as a fear of unstable heterosexuality – in the arts, in politics, and in private life. Consider the dashing President Reagan in flashy cowboy regalia alongside, say, the androgynous Axl Rose,

Street brawl or rough sex?

front man for heavy metal band Guns N' Roses, with rail-thin frame, shrinkwrapped leather pants and terrifically teased hair (see inside the dust jacket of Guns N' Roses' debut album, *Appetite for Destruction*). Each epitomised specific and *oppositional* types of mediatised maleness in the 1980s, imagistically and rhetorically.[29] Still, both icons, in these guises at least, would qualify as 'gay chic' in some circles.

There is also something to be said for the meta-homoerotic implications of *They Live*'s fight/fuck scene vis-à-vis the long history of 'pro wrestling's flaming love affair with all things queer' and the notion that the sport is 'simultaneously homoerotic and homophobic' (Vadim 2000).[30] In *Uncyclopedia*, for instance, a satirical version of *Wikipedia*, 'professional wrestling' is defined as 'the primary leisure activity of the American repressed homosexual, just ahead of the NFL, being a douchebag, and membership in the Republican party'. The entry is silly but contains a seed of truth, indicting the heterosexuality of pro-wrestlers and people who watch them. In its historical context, the equally silly fight/fuck scene points a finger at the dubious sexuality and hypermasculinity of Nada-Piper, a totemic and multi-narrational phallus. More importantly, it implicates male viewers who went to see *They Live* because they were such big fans of Piper and pro wrestling. Masculine spectators thus become voyeurs ogling the spectacle of their own precarious masculinity.

For all these reasons, I want to put forward that the scene in question, a paradoxically disposable yet indispensable display of *variance*, represents what amounts to a zeitgeist of violence and fetishised masculinity in the 1980s. It is the most transgressive display in *They Live* by dint of its narrative variation from 'reality' into irreality. It is doubly transgressive in its variation of normative heterosexuality, underscoring the forces of male insecurity that authorise the diegeses of the film and the real world.

Moreover, *They Live* addresses a racial dilemma that, like sexuality, plays out in the relationship between Nada and Armitage and crests in the fight scene. Armitage resists Nada from the beginning; he resists Nada's nosiness, his compulsion to seek out the truth, and during the fight, he resists Nada's insistence on wearing the sunglasses, literal and symbolic instruments of perception. Literally, as we know, the sunglasses will show him the black-and-white reality that lurks behind the colourful curtain of capitalist illusion. Symbolically, they reminisce the power struggles of American slavery, as Lethem advises:

> If we're not utterly race blind, there's a special poignancy at the lengths of Frank's resistance to the wake-up call. No white outlaw is going to tell this black worker how to protect his family! Frank defends a middle-class self-definition against a lower-order point of view, even if it's the truth. African-Americans might find that the view through the Hoffman lenses offers an unbearable degree of indignity: Still a slave, fool. Still a fool, slave. (2010: 119)

Viewed in this light, Armitage's obduracy becomes much

more than a means for Carpenter to stage a lengthy brawl. Nada converts into the white master attempting to force his viewpoint onto the black slave. He may be trying to educate Armitage, rather than keep him ignorant and 'happy', as was the custom of most Antebellum slaveowners who disallowed their slaves from learning how to read.[31] The authority of Nada's aggression, however, far exceeds his alleged objective; after all, he threatens to beat Armitage if he doesn't listen to him and bow to his will. His objective is questionable anyway. Does he genuinely care about Armitage and have his best interests in mind, or does he simply not want to be the only one who can see the aliens and their subliminal signage? Conceivably Nada just wants somebody to help him satisfy his desire to 'win' (i.e. to *compensate*), which he feels unable to do by himself. African-Americans bear a long tradition of 'helping' white people achieve their goals, and at their own expense. It pans out in the film: Armitage dies but not before subordinating Nada in 'saving the world'. Given this tradition, Armitage's defiance seems rational. It is perhaps only under the basest auspices of American history that it *could* be rational as opposed to a mere vehicle for Carpenter's spectacle.

They Live is a movie about *exposure*. Exposure to class divisions. Exposure to racial trauma. Exposure to enemies of the body and of consciousness. Exposure to patriarchal authorities. Most of all, exposure to the various realities that activate the human condition. Hence: *over*exposure. The Hoffmen lenses represent the convergence of this affliction. The *mise-en-scènes* that they reveal look like overexposed photographs, whitewashed of colour, stripped of finer nuances. In terms of race, it is crucial that reality avails itself in black-and-white, laying bare the spectre of racial conflict that, at the very least, undergirds and empowers Nada vs. Armitage. More imperative is the issue of violence. Psychologically, ideologically, symbolically and physically, *They Live*'s overexposure of violent outbreaks trumps all other issues and constitutes the thematic heartbeat of the film.

In *Violence*, Slavoj Žižek identifies two kinds of violence, 'subjective' and 'objective'. Subjective violence comprises visible acts 'performed by a clearly identifiable agent' (2008: 1), meaning acts of violence committed by and between *subjects*, socially constructed and interpellated individuals and communities. Objective violence is 'invisible' and comprises the symbolic – 'violence embodied in language and its forms' (2008: 2) – and the systemic – 'the often catastrophic consequences of the smooth functioning of our economic and political systems' (ibid.). These abstract forms supplement 'real' or physical violence, 'acts of crime and terror, civil unrest, international conflict' (2008: 1). All of them coexist at the narrative vanguard of *They Live*. Citing Guy Debord and Louis Althusser, I discussed in chapter four how Nada and others are ideologically produced as social bodies by oppressive capitalist forces – the quintessence of subjective violence in the film. Symbolic violence manifests most clearly in the subliminal messages (a language of capital) that the aliens hide behind the signs of consumerism and urbanity for the purposes of forcing the human masses into oneiric submission. We see overt systemic violence in *They Live*'s intricate and politically-charged critique of Reaganism. And there is extensive physical violence, the fight scene above all, but also the police raid on Justiceville, Nada's shooting sprees, the mnemonic image of his father's abuse, the jolting image of Holly braining him and Nada crashing out a window, and so on. Nada's verbal tirades pack a wallop, too. Violent acts of both weird and believable calibers pervade the film and either stem from or surround the protagonist, whose arrival in Los Angeles (and the cinematic diegesis) sets the wheels of rack-and-ruin in motion. In his absence, presumably things would have remained 'peaceful', which is to say, violence would have been relegated to its subjective, symbolic and systemic forms.

In the epilogue of his book, Žižek indicates that violence, exhibited in films like *Taxi Driver* (1976) and *The Fugitive* (1993) as well as the Chinese Cultural Revolution and Nazi Germany, often originates in a *passage a l'acte*, an impulsive and compensatory reaction to some kind of (authentic or mis-perceived) antagonism against the (individual or collective) self. These reactions are chronically impotent; their execution solves nothing. We could say the same thing about Nada's own violent *passage a l'acte*, whether what happens in the film is 'real' or a pathological wish-fulfilment fantasy unfold-ing onto his mindscreen. We don't know what happens af-ter Nada destroys the signal. We know that humans can see aliens *au naturel* now. Should we assume, say, that humans will promptly revolt against their masters? Complements of Nada, will 'the violent overthrow of the bourgeoisie lay … the foundation for the sway of the proletariat' (Marx 1978: 483)? More likely, the aliens will reinstall the signal and society will return to business as usual. In any event, all we can be sure of at the conclusion of *They Live* is Nada's death – literal, metaphorical, or both – and the bruises, the bullet holes, the echoes of rants and wisecracks he leaves behind him.

6

LEGACIES

FINAL (OVER)EXPOSURES

In the aftermath of Nada and Armitage's decidedly mutual asskicking, *They Live* feels a lot like anticlimax. Over thirty minutes remain. Despite plenty of blazing gunfire and some key expository dialogue, at no point does the film accomplish such a level of uncanniness, badness and wistful ferocity as it does during Carpenter's homage to pro wrestling.

Nada and Armitage never become bosom buddies, but they do become brothers-in-arms. Hiding out at a hotel, they encounter Gilbert, one of Justiceville's rebel leaders. He tips them off to a secret meeting where fellow humans conspire to overthrow the aliens. Holly shows up, and afterwards so do the cops. They massacre most of the rebels with shotguns and Uzis. Nada and Armitage shoot their way out and unintentionally open a portal in an alleyway that leads them to a labyrinth beneath the city – the aliens' underground 'lair'. Skirting soldiers on patrol, Nada and Armitage discover a lavish dinner party in an enormous Victorian ballroom attended by aliens and, as the keynote speaker calls them, the 'human power elite' (alien friendlies). Among the elite is the Drifter, who recognises Nada and Armitage from Justiceville. In spite of their ragtag attire, he welcomes them 'aboard' and proceeds to give them a tour of 'backstage at the show'. We learn more about the aliens here than anywhere else in the film (motives, methods, intents). The Drifter's tour concludes just outside Cable 54 in the control room that generates the master signal. Nada and Armitage kill two guards and storm the TV studio. Aided by Hoffman contact lenses, they can see alien and human employees, and they blast their way to the roof. Near the top they find Holly; frenzied now, Nada drags her along with them. In a service staircase, Nada aerates a group of soldiers and scurries up the last steps onto the roof, shouting for his companions to follow. Before Armitage can comply, Holly pulls a handgun from skintight jeans, puts it to his temple and pulls the trigger.

Beneath the night sky, Holly confronts Nada, assuring him, just as the Drifter did, that he 'can't win'. A helicopter appears and Nada is ordered to stand down. He shoots Holly, shoots the satellite, and the soldiers in the helicopter shoot him. Pyrotechnics ensue – the satellite goes up in sparks and flames, and just before he dies, Nada gives the occupants of the helicopter the finger, a final 'Fuck You' to the symbolic father that produced him.

The last seconds bring the theme of overexposure in *They Live* to a head as the aliens are revealed, primarily on television screens, in their true 'formaldehyde face' forms. We see ghoulish newscasters and talking heads, one of which makes a brazen meta-comment: 'All the sex and violence on the screen has gone too far for me. I'm fed up with it. Filmmakers like George Romero and John Carpenter have to show some restraint.' In the closing shot, a bare-breasted woman, eyes closed, rides somebody cowgirl-style. We can't see her part-

Nada gives the finger to the aliens – and, by extension, to the audience.

ner. A poster that reads MARRY AND REPRODUCE hangs on the wall behind her, and on the TV at the foot of the bed, a car commercial shows, among other things, the headlight on a sports coupé opening up and turning on (i.e. *awakening*) as a deep, manly, affected voice delivers the pitch, which capital-izes on the themes of masculinity and power that have run throughout the film: "You're filled with lightning when you hit the road. You're feeling that V-6 power and you take con-trol. Nothing can stop you now." The commercial ends when a man in a suit with his back to the camera is slapped in the face by a woman in a dress. As she strides away, the man turns to the camera and we realize he is an alien. He gasps as if he knows that we can see him. The bare-breasted woman turns her eyes from the TV to her partner – who she, like us, realizes is an alien, too. Puzzled, the alien lifts his head off the bed and says, 'Hey, what's wrong, baby?' Roll credits.

Channelling gratuitous gore (close-ups on slimy skull-faces), sexuality (shots of the woman's breasts, the only occasion of nudity in the film) and an air of self-consciousness (the talk-ing head's critique of Carpenter's cinematic excess), this final meta-narrational bodyslam hearkens back to the multiplicity of meta-narrations that invigorate the film and express that, for better and for worse, Carpenter 'knows what he's doing', critiquing late-1980s, Cold War, consumer-capitalist culture for the mediatised, misogynistic 'business' that it is. The exploitation of naked breasts as a metaphor for 'seeing', 'truth', 'wakefulness' or 'consciousness' verifies a crisis of male desire and incriminates the male gaze. The breasts are an adolescent jab, but not without rhyme and reason. In fact, they may just signify, once and for all, the film's ascendant thesis: the problem with society, specifically the violent nature of social conduct, now and throughout history, is *men*. Hence the *They* of the film's title are *masculine subjects in power*. The thesis clashes with Carpenter's *modus operandi*, here and in most of his films, which takes noted pleasure in violence and aggressive masculine play, endorsing the exploits of masculine subjects. His critique of 1980s culture and the primacy of capitalist patriarchy and class divisions collapses upon itself, as does the notion that he 'knows what he's doing'. *They Live* reaffirms masculinity with one hand and undermines it with the other, rendering Carpenter's would-be wake-up call profoundly inane – not because of dumb artifices like Hoffman lenses, but because of gender technicalities. In terms of its cult status, this is perhaps the film's greatest transgression: *an attempt to make a serious critique, the effects of which rupture into boyish goofiness. They Live* wants much more than it can possibly deliver, and the exposed breasts represent nothing short of an orgasmic insignia of the film's spectacular failure.

Removed from this gendered analysis, Robert Cumbow contends: 'The last shot, of a naked couple making love, and the human woman suddenly seeing for the first time the true face of her alien lover, is a clever sight gag of an ending. But it also makes us wonder about the extent to which the aliens have already inbred with earth people, and recognize that in the future, it may be even *harder* to tell them from us' (2000: 178). As mentioned before, the future is ambiguous.

The traditional meat-and-potatoes narrative dies with Nada. Which is to say, it *closes* with his death, and successive footage moves *They Live* into the postmodern landscape. 'These two are lost somewhere in the breach between the TV satires and their own longing for authentic contact, *fucking with the TV on*, or *watching TV with the fucking on*, their behavior mediated through porn stylistics that have invaded their sexual imaginations' (Lethem 2010: 156). On this level, too, the scene points backwards, now to the thematic strain of the ways television and other electronic media mediatises/pathologises postmodern capitalist subjectivity.

From a theoretical perspective, the film, empowered by lingering postmodern affinities, resists coming to a tightly sealed conclusion. Carpenter's use of Nada-Piper as a political tool achieves a special failure. According to the theory of Michel Foucault, 'there is no single privileged place for the political activist to go to work, no locus of power whose removal will bring the whole system tumbling down' (Simon 2001: 1618). If so, no matter what Nada does, he will not 'win' – the Drifter and Holly were right, in more ways than one – and he was doomed to oblivion from the start. The signification of his middle finger – understanding the direction in which he points his terminal 'Fuck You' – is not simply at alien oppression, but at the system that fails him by default. It is also directed at viewers, perhaps more than anybody. As subjects who purchase tickets and go to the movies, they support the reign of consumer media and capitalist pathology; as such, *They* are the 'real' alien capitalists. *The aliens are us.*[32]

Speaking more practically, the idea that the film dies/closes with Nada suggests that *They Live* could be a simple wish-fulfilment fantasy, Nada's dream of manifesting a heroic persona in order to save the world, and thus himself, from the evils of class divisions and patriarchal construction. He dies in the dream, and in the wake of his dawning consciousness, all that remains are mediatised traces of masculine excess and desire…

THE LOSS OF *THEY LIVE*

Whether they are cinephiliacs, buffs or casual viewers, and whether they saw the film in the twentieth or the twenty-first century, audiences seem to remember the fight scene between Nada and Armitage more than anything about *They Live*. In effect, it has achieved the status of cult legend in and of itself. Again, the scene was, among other things, an explicit ode on Carpenter's part to the faux violence of professional wrestling. It still works that way, although its impact has weathered over the years as the actors have grown older and drifted away from the popular consciousness. Nobody really knew who Keith David was in the first place – his name, at least – even though he has been recognizable in prominent supporting roles, on big and small screens, and in nearly two hundred shows, movies and video games of varying genres and success rates; as he closes on sixty, he is busier than ever, appearing in multiple titles in 2013 and 2014 alone. Piper has appeared in almost sixty shows, films and video games, mostly B-movie schlock, and as he eclipses sixty, he seems less recognizable. (Whereas David looks more or less like he did 25 years ago, only with greying hair, Piper looks quite different – noticeably aged and overweight with a receding hairline and tattered goatee – almost like another person). Additionally, Piper has been reduced to making regular appearances at horror and wrestling conventions, presumably to pay the bills. David, in turn, enjoys a surplus of work purely onscreen, in person and doing voice-overs for which he has received multiple Emmy awards, his crisp baritone recalling the vocal prowess of Orson Welles and James Earle Jones. Despite their differences and quantity of output, however, both actors still tend to be most associated with their roles in *They Live* and Carpenter's over-the-top fight sequence, which, since its inception, is still used as a gauge for movie brawls that have followed it.

Virtually every comprehensive list of 'best fight scenes' I have seen includes *They Live. Rotten Tomatoes*' 'Total Recall: The 20 Greatest Fight Scenes Ever' and *Progressive Boink*'s 'The 50 Greatest Fight Scenes of Film' both rank Nada vs. Armitage at number seven, *Moviefone*'s 'Top 25 Fight Scenes' at number five, and *The Schiznit*'s 'Top 50 Movie Fight Scenes' at number 16. In *Paste Magazine*'s 'The Thirty Best Fight Scenes in Movie History', Josh Jackson places it at number twelve and writes: 'The fight is great, but the fact that it's over Keith David's refusal to wear a pair of sunglasses is even greater. And despite having just punched David in the crotch, the only thing Rowdy Roddy Piper apologizes for is accidentally breaking his car window'. All of the fights on these lists make it for one of two reasons: humor and absurdity, or seriousness and grit. Nada vs. Armitage is one of the few scenes that unites *both* frameworks in equal measure, and even list-makers who hate the film can't resist situating the fight within the annals of Hollywood cinema.[33]

Despite the trivialisation of the texts they mock, spoofs function as badges of honour insofar as they indicate that a text has 'succeeded', garnering a wide appeal and ingraining itself into mass consciousness. Blockbuster financial returns tend to ensue, but not always. *They Live*'s 'success' was confirmed with a spoof in 2001 when the animated adult American sitcom *South Park* aired 'Cripple Fight'. In this episode, two disabled children, crutch-hampered Jimmy and wheelchair-confined Timmy, engage in a blow-by-blow, grunt-by-grunt re-enactment of the fight between Nada and Armitage that, as co-producers Matt Stone and Trey Parker say on the DVD commentary, was animated to the soundtrack. There is even a YouTube video that superimposes the *South Park* soundtrack onto the original film. The dialogue isn't the same – the only word Timmy can articulate is his name, typically with croaking enthusiasm. But nearly all of the other features match up, down to the sound of Nada's fist connecting with Armitage's jaw, and vice versa. The primary intention here is to be funny. Interestingly, the parody does not accentuate the melodramatic nature of its source, as is often the case. Instead it reminds us how silly the source was in the first place. It also tells us that the original itself was a simulacra, lampooning professional wrestling (if only by representation), which lampoons 'real' fighting, and outdoing cinematic fights (such as the one in *The Quiet Man*) that preceded it.

Furthermore, 'Cripple Fight' has superseded *They Live* in the megatext of popular culture. Based on what I have read in personal and professional blogs and reviews, teenagers and twentysomethings know about 'Cripple Fight', but they don't necessarily know about *They Live*, other than that's where 'Cripple Fight' came from, and they aren't really interested in seeing the original, as if Carpenter's version has died and its ghost has returned to haunt us in an incurably absurd form. So

Jimmy and Timmy parody the already parodic Nada and Armitage.

the parody achieves primacy over the subject of its comedic meta-attack, a not uncommon upshot. As Mikhail Bakhtin suggests in *The Dialogic Imagination*, parody is the natural end-product of any textual line of flight where the original traditionally belongs to 'high' cultural discourse, the parodied to 'low' (1981: 76). A good example is *Airplane!* (1980), the classic politically incorrect slapstick riff on the airborne disaster films *Zero Hour* (1957) and the *Airport* tetralogy, all mainstream dramas that met with commercial success.[34] It is *Airplane!*, however, that sticks in modern American memory in both cult and mainstream circles. For the past three decades, it has been played and replayed on multiple television channels and arguably gave birth to the salvo of bastardised spoofs that have inundated the twenty-first-century market, such as *Not Another Teen Movie* (2001), *Meet the Spartans* (2008) and the *Scary Movie* franchise (2000–13), films that fit readily into the keyhole of trash culture. *Airport*, on the other hand, despite being called trashy by some critics, received an Academy Award nomination for Best Picture and has been called the 'granddaddy of disaster flicks' (Weinberg 2005).[35] But how do we account for *They Live,* the street fight and the movie as a whole, which was, true to much of Carpenter's oeuvre, 'low' to begin with? Does 'Cripple Fight' acknowledge the cult status of *They Live* by way of its terrific badness? Or does the *South Park* episode accomplish the very opposite, indicting a film that didn't merit interest in the first place aside from one weird, brutal and protracted scene?

Cult films are almost never spoofed. They aren't well-known enough to be spoof-worthy, and they share a distinct sense of play with the genre, even if they aren't normally hardline parodies themselves. It seems that the best cult films try to be 'serious' and fail on numerous levels of narrative and cinematic execution; absurdist humour results, as evinced in, say, *The Man Who Fell to Earth* (1976) and *Showgirls* (1995). On the other end of the spectrum are films that actively pursue cult aesthetics, revelling in camp, gore, ultraviolence, intertextuality and transgression, as we see in touchstones like *The Rocky Horror Picture Show* and *Bad Taste* (1985). As departures from the mainstream, all cult films are unique. *They Live* is unique within the cult genre, too, occupying both ends of the spectrum. It attempts to be serious, for the most part, as a dramatic narrative and a source of social and political propaganda. At the same time, Carpenter knowingly makes use of cult tropes, attitudes and oddities that recur again and again in his cinema. This inherent irony extends to the film's dominant theme of masculine economy that the director simultaneously problematises, jeopardises, satirises ... and glorifies. As a social and cultural formation, masculinity undergoes a process of reification and destabilisation. This can be attributed to a wilful ethos of play, but there is also a sense of confusion and uncertainty, specifically regarding the state of male identity as produced by *the cult of the 1980s*, an ironic decade in itself, or at least a decade scarred by conflicting forces. On my own mindscreen, when I visualise the 1980s, I am haunted by figments of red dawns and mushroom clouds, yet enamoured by images of hair bands, arcade games and Rubik's Cubes, the latter group representing a jubilant and colourful *mode de vie*, the former representing the end of civilisation. For me, *They Live* will always embody a conflation (and *conflagration*) of fun and terror as a piece of cinema and an extrapolation of reality.

Cult films take many forms and can differ from one another in extreme ways. It poses a problem for the burgeoning field of cult studies and the effort to analyse and quantify them. Part of the difficulty is that they can fall into any genre or combination of genres. The cyberpunk Japanimé *Akira* (1988), for instance, is at odds with its musical cult peer *The Sound of Music* (1965), a far cry from *Akira* in virtually every way, just as both films are a far cry from the vulgar, surreal Scottish drama *Trainspotting* (1996) and the dreamy, moody, 'anti-film' *Eraserhead* (1977). But all of these examples share a devoted fan base – the foremost component of cult cinema. 'In the cinema the term "cult" tends to be used rather loosely', writes Barry Grant, 'to describe a variety of films, old and new, that are extremely popular or have a particularly devoted audience' (2008: 77). On a textual level, Grant identifies an element of transgression and an 'embrace of "badness"' as the common cult thread (2008: 78). In *Cult Films: Taboo and Transgression*, Allan Havis concurs, but he uses the term 'decadence', a means of embracing the 'other' that includes three practices: 1) a fashionable degeneration following periods of high artistic success and novelty; 2) a rejection of dominant moral imperatives; and 3) an attempt to use strange, often unrealistic methods to come to a more interesting and seasoned understanding of reality and truth (as opposed to the understanding achieved by 'realism') (2007: 3).

Even *The Sound of Music* is decadent. The film has become such a familiar staple of American culture that its cult affiliations go unnoticed. As a child in the 1970s – long before VCRs, DVD players, On Demand and Netflix – I remember what a big event television showings of *The Sound of Music* were for my family, and it still gets played on TV a lot today. Besides its badness (e.g. weird, watered-down representations of Naziism and reality in general, even for a musical),[36] the film 'overplays the emotional states of characters and situations', incites nostalgia 'for the glamour and picturesque scenery of traditional Austria' and displays a 'sense of communion and community' with the Von Trapps many singalongs (Mathijs & Mendik 2008: 2, 3, 4). Hyperbolic emotion, nostalgia and community – these elements attest to the cult standing of *The Sound of Music*.

There is no question about *They Live*'s celebration of badness and decadence. Even though Carpenter's film is profoundly different than *The Sound of Music*, however, it exhibits the same cult traits. Emotional excess materialises both in Nada's volatile temperament (compliments of Nada-Piper) and the paranoid Cold War society that the film extrapolates. *They Live* creates nostalgia through the homage it pays to classic sci-fi cinema like *It Came from Outer Space* (1953), *Invaders from Mars* (1953) and *Forbidden Planet* (1956).[37] And it immediately established a two-fold community of ready-at-the-helm devotees who were either already devoted to Carpenter's canon or to Roddy Piper's pro wrestling persona. I was certainly a member of these communities before the release of *They Live*, although I no longer watch or even like wrestling, and I have been consistently disappointed with Carpenter's films since *They Live*, which, for me, marks the end of his most compelling work in genre cinema.

In other words, I have not 'lost' *They Live*. But what about its place in the wider sphere of culture? Younger generations often dictate American cultural form, production and memory, and unlike many cult films, *They Live* does not seem to have been favourably passed down the line. Except for the fight scene, immortalised by cartoon satire, it has been, to some degree, 'lost'. What does that mean in terms of its cult identity? What about cult films in general? If it disappears, was it ever a cult phenomenon to begin with? Bear in mind: *They Live* is an anomaly in the genre. Most cult films develop a viewership over time. *They Live*, on the contrary, *began* as a cult film, thanks to the reputation of its director, and since it came out, its fan base has steadily dwindled.

Perhaps the remake of *They Live* will settle the score. It has been in the works, on and off, since I began research for this volume in 2009. As of late 2014, the remake is listed as 'in development' on IMDb, but there is no information about plot or casting. Many of Carpenter's films have gained new life through remakes, including *Assault on Precinct 13* (2005), *The Fog* (2005) and *Halloween* (2007), all of which met with some critical and viewer acclaim, yet mainly generated praise for the original films. Remakes update narratives and/or wield new age special effects in order to, per usual, make money. Inevitably deviations from the original films occur. These deviations can set fans of the originals aflame with dread and enmity, but sometimes it's hard to gauge how a remake will reinvigorate or reinvent its source. As the title of the 2011 article, '*They Live* Remake Isn't a Remake: Matt Reeves to Direct *8 O'Clock In The Morning*', suggests, *They Live* will not be based on Carpenter's film, but on Ray Nelson's short story and subsequent comic. Reeves observes that 'Carpenter took a satirical view of the material and the larger political implication that we're being controlled. I am very drawn to the emotional side, the nightmare experience with the paranoia of *Invasion of the Body Snatchers* or a Roman Polanski-style film' (quoted in Tommy 2011).

The (non)remake, then, will be a kind of a negation, not simply a deviation. This approach may bode poorly or do wonders for the future of the original *They Live*. Then again, the film might simply stay where it lays – an elegy to the 1980s, to Carpenter (still alive, but professionally dead, or in hibernation), and to the hard rubber fist of American patriarchy and masculinity (also still alive, but in an altered, possibly more dangerous guise). Regardless of its following, in the past or in the future, *They Live* has the capacity to stand with the giants of cult cinema and could function as a primer for studies of the form precisely because it *succeeds* so effectively at *failing* to be what it wants (and doesn't want) to be.

NOTES

1   Reagan's favoring of the rich was epitomised by his 'trickle-down economics' policy, which provided tax exemptions to the upper classes in the hope that it would indirectly benefit the wider population. It didn't. Feinstein explains the policy in greater depth: 'President Reagan believed that, if taxes were lowered, people – especially the wealthy – would have more spare funds and would invest more money in corporations. If American businesses prospered as a result, they would, in turn, create more jobs and give pay raises to their employees. This was seen as a "trickle-down" effect that would help poor people. So in 1981 and again in 1986, Reagan reduced rates for corporate and personal income taxes. "Reaganomics", as this economic policy was called, was criticized by many as unfair to the poor. Many complained that the benefits never actually "trickled down" far enough to help lower-income people. However, Reaganomics was extremely popular among the yuppies and with businesspeople to whom it gave financial advantages' (2006: 37). In 1988, at the end of his second term, Reagan left the federal government over two trillion dollars in debt.

2   Jack Boozer addresses these issues in more detail: 'The two … major scandals surrounding the Reagan presidency were financial ones. The first problem really began in 1980 and continued to worsen throughout the decade. The savings and loan system was originally created to promote housing and home ownership, but when it ran into problems during the high inflation years of the early 1980s, the federal government began deregulating it and giving it increased government-backed insurance coverage, more lenient

accounting standards, and an expansion of the types of banking activities it could undertake. By 1986 the Government Accounting Office estimated that the loss to government S&L insurance funds had reached $20 billion. If the government had acted on this at that time, the red ink might have been stopped. Instead of controlling the problem, however, Congress passed a bill in August 1987 … that authorized a $10.8 billion recapitalization of the Federal Savings and Loan Insurance Commission, including forbearance measures designed to postpone or prevent S&L closures … Reagan's policies have been most frequently faulted for increasing the national debt, which in many ways was symbolized by his failure to control the growing S&L problem' (2007: 173).

3   Schwarzenegger has repeatedly admitted to steroid use. Following a 2007 arrest for possession of HGH (Human Growth Hormone) in Australia, Stallone confessed to using the drug (technically not a steroid) for years, championing its health benefits. Whatever the case, as artificial, body-enhancing substances that compensate for a corporeal lack, steroids and HGH contribute to the hyperreal status of the Schwarzenegger/Stallone monster-hero, who is a caricatured, parodic representation of desire. This representation is verified by the ultraviolence the monster-hero inflicts in addition to the hyperreal medium of cinema in which that ultraviolence is enacted.

4   In science fiction cinema, the expression 'desert of the real' (and Baudrillard himself) is more commonly associated with the Wachowskis' *Matrix* trilogy (1999–2003), films that overtly employ themes of hyperreality and simulacra. We are even shown a copy of *Simulacra & Simulation* in the first instalment. The *Matrix* trilogy owes much to *They Live*, which tells a similar story *sans* glitzy, high-tech special effects, and which refigures artificial intelligences in the role of the aliens.

5   Baudrillard is among the most prolific postmodern theorists and provocateurs. Throughout his work, he levels a critique of image-culture at America and the global projection of American ideology, media and capitalism. Disneyland in the 1970s and 1980s was the criterion site of hyperreality gone awry. 'Disneyland', Baudrillard writes, 'is presented as imaginary in order to make us believe that the real is real, whereas all of Los Angeles and the America that surrounds it are no longer real, but belong to the hyperreal order

and to the order of simulation' (2000: 12). This is the categorical state of affairs in *They Live* – literally and metaphorically, ideologically and ontologically, socially and metaphysically.

6   Based on Peter George's more serious novel *Red Alert* (1958), Kubrick's comedic film satirises the Cold War at a time when it was gaining impetus in the American consciousness in the middle of the Vietnam War (1955–75). Shone's allusion intimately connects the rise of the blockbuster film with the (anti)climax of the Cold War in the 1980s.

7   Foremost among these critics is Peter Biskind, whose *Easy Riders, Raging Bulls: How the Sex-Drugs-and-Rock 'N' Roll Generation Saved Hollywood* (2011) Shone writes against.

8   In *The Society of the Spectacle* (1967), Debord rethinks and restylises Marx's theory of commodity fetishism in terms of postmodern media and technoculture. He emphasises how the commodity of the image, in its various and proliferating forms, pathologises subjectivity.

9   Truffaut prefaces his article with the following statement of intent: 'These notes have no object other than to define a certain tendency of French cinema, a tendency spoken of as psychological realism and to sketch out some of its limitations' (2008: 9). His scope proves to be much wider, more political and antagonistic, as he rejects 'the literary films of the "Tradition of Quality" in favor of a *cinéma des auteurs* in which filmmakers like Jean Renoir and Jean Cocteau express a more personal vision' (ibid.).

10   In *The Films of John Carpenter* (2000), John Muir talks about Carpenter's frustrations with Hollywood following the box office failure of *Big Trouble in Little China*: 'Upon introspection, Carpenter realized that the best experiences of his life had been those times in which he had been *outside* the studio system, making small films with complete autonomy. … Making a bold decision, Carpenter stepped back from Hollywood and returned to the independent arena […] Stung by his experiences with *The Thing*, *Christine*, *Starman* and *Big Trouble in Little China*, as well as the marketing of his name on *The Philadelphia Experiment* and *Black Moon Rising*, Carpenter in early 1987 signed a four-film package deal with Alive Films, the small company that had produced *Kiss of the Spider Woman* (1985) … as well as *The Whales of August* (1986). Alive Film's two executive gurus, Andre Blay and Shep Gordon, wanted Carpenter

to make films for them, and Carpenter appreciated the freedom they were willing to extend to him. ... Because autonomy was something important to Carpenter (as it was to his hero, Howard Hawks), the Alive Films deal was perfect' (2000: 37). *They Live* was the second film made under the auspices of this deal after *Prince of Darkness* (1987). Originally Alive Films, a subsidiary of Universal Studios, signed Carpenter on for four movies, allocating $3 million apiece to the director on the condition that the he have complete autonomy (see Boulenger 2001: 201). Poor returns prompted Universal to back out after the second instalment.

11 We are not told what circumstances led George Nada to a stage hypnotist – presumably an evening of idle entertainment. The hypnotist is merely a narrative vehicle for his awakening. Nelson uses the same vehicle at the beginning of his story.

12 As in *They Live*, this process of revolution is theoretically Marxist with the Fascinators cast in the mould of the bourgeois and the humans in the mould of the proletariat. But the dynamics of class and capitalism are more pronounced in the film.

13 Capitalism as a systemic manifestation of desire is an *idée fixe* in Deleuze and Guattari's books on capitalism and schizophrenia, *Anti-Oedipus* (1972) and *A Thousand Plateaus* (1980), translations of which were first published in the US in the 1980s. Guattari makes clear how it works in *Chaosophy*: 'Of course, capitalism was and remains a formidable desiring machine. The monetary flux, the means of production, of manpower, of new markets, all that is the flow of desire. It's enough to consider the sum of contingencies at the origin of capitalism to see to what degree it has been a crossroads of desires, and that its infrastructure, even its economy, was inseparable from the phenomena of desire' (1995: 63). Of particular interest about this theory in connection with *They Live* is that it implicates the human as an alien, the self as an other. As I will discuss later, Deleuze and Guattari invite us to read the film as a projection of Nada's broken and schizophrenised unconscious.

14 In the wake of *They Live*, Piper has appeared and starred in many films and television shows. Most of them fall into B-movie terrain, including titles such as *Immortal Combat* (1994), *Jungleground* (1995), *Legless Larry & the Lipstick Lady* (1999) and *Costa Chica: Confession of an Exorcist* (2006).

15 Justiceville was an actual place established and subsequently de-

molished in 1985. 'Justiceville, the activism of JHUSA (Justiceville/ Homeless, USA), is the non-profit … corporation at the root of Dome Village's existence. Initiated by homeless activist Ted Hayes, Justiceville was born in January 1985 during [the] time of a conservative controlled federal government. It began as a tidy shantytown in the heart of Central City East, otherwise known as Skid Row. Organized by more than 73 residents, Justiceville's diverse population consisted of men, women and children of various ethnicities and even welcomed their pets. Under Ted Hayes' leadership and a small core of village residents, Justiceville became the first community of homeless people of its kind in the County of Los Angeles. Shortly after its inception the homeless village became a media hit, with news outlets capturing its saga of surviving against all odds. Those odds were a consequence of social service providers, advocates and a mayor who viewed the shanty community as a threat to the status quo of political arrangements in the city. The strained relations between the popular community, social service providers and the imminent threat of closure by the authorities, led Ted Hayes to enter a fast that lasted a total of 35 days that ended only upon the closure of the Justiceville shantytown on May 10, 1985' ('History of JHUSA'). Both the real Justiceville and Carpenter's version possess elements of utopia and dystopia. And both end in the latter.

16 Harrington pans nearly every Carpenter film he reviews for the *Washington Post*, experiencing a palpable *jouissance* in berating them, but also a kind of lament for Carpenter's earlier work. As he writes in the first lines of a review of *Village of the Damned* (1995): 'Has Carpenter lost his mind or his talent? On the heel of *In the Mouth of Madness* comes the director's rehash of the 1960s classic … Unfortunately Carpenter simply makes a hash of it.'

17 As Ernest Mathijs and Xavier Mendik indicate, 'the genres that cult cinema is mostly associated with are popular ones, like the horror film, science fiction, and fantasy – three genres that rely heavily upon formalized story worlds hugely different from reality, but which are also extremely coherent internally – as such they provide worlds one can get lost in or expand upon' (2008: 15).

18 The failure of *Memoirs of an Invisible Man* was mostly Chevy Chase's fault. In the early 1990s, Chase had reached the apex of his career as a comedic actor. He purchased the rights to H.F. Saint's

1987 mystery novel of the same name in an attempt to, says Carpenter, 'start a career as a more serious actor – and that was the problem. We tried to straddle the line and it didn't work. It did not work! He was the star and took the fall when the movie was not a big hit, so in a way he showed courage. He still sends me a Christmas card every year' (quoted in Boulenger 2001: 220). In the past, Carpenter had successfully interwoven comedy and drama, as in *They Live*, but also *Big Trouble in Little China* and his first feature film, *Dark Star* (1974). He sculpted these films from beginning to end himself, however, having creative control.

19   This percentage was recorded in January 2011.

20   Mathijs and Mendik claim that *The Wizard of Oz*'s 'openness to multiple allegorical interpretations has given it cultural weight and a cult reputation' (2008: 9). Naturally there are lots of other inter- and extra-textual factors, such as the way the film entered the popular consciousness. Barely surpassing its production and distribution costs at the box office, *The Wizard of Oz* did not establish itself as a cult phenomenon until years later through television exposure.

21   Lethem ascribes a much wider relevance to the sunglasses as chronic signifiers of 1980s capitalist media culture: 'Ray-Ban Wayfarers, which convey an iconographic lineage back to J.F.K. and Marilyn Monroe, as well as Audrey Hepburn in *Breakfast at Tiffany's* and Cary Grant in *North by Northwest*, had been established as a specifically 1980s movie icon by a crushingly effective product-placement campaign begun in 1982; after Tom Cruise's use of the glasses in *Risky Business* (1983) and Don Johnson's in *Miami Vice* (1984–89), and then with their adoption by the music icons Michael Jackson and Debbie Harry, and in the texts and jacket designs of the novels of Bret Easton Ellis, the glasses were an 1980s cliché no one was ever embarrassed to deploy' (2010: 57).

22   Hence Marx's disclaimer: 'The criticism of religion is, therefore, *in embryo, the criticism of that vale of tears* of which religion is the *halo*' (1978: 54).

23   I should note that 'capitalist servitude' is contingent upon an illusion of transcendence. Despite what it claims to be, capitalism as a system can only function in pyramid form, with a small group at the top owning and controlling most of the resources while the majority of subjects (re)jockey for position beneath them, thinking that they, too, can rise to the top, given the proper work ethic and

quantity of 'luck'. Of course, if everybody rose to the top (or vice versa) the system would collapse. Capitalism keeps itself in place by the perpetuation of a dangling carrot, and generally people are born and die within the same social and economic strata. There are exceptions to the rule – there must be. And they must be seen and heard, showing the masses how they have mastered the system, thus prompting the masses to spin the wheels of the pyramid's undercarriage harder. Gilles Deleuze theorises this prescription in 'Capitalism: A Very Special Delirium', underlining its pathological logic: 'Underneath all reason lies delirium, drift. Everything is rational in capitalism, except capital and capitalism itself. The stock market is certainly rational; one can understand it, study it, the capitalists know how to use it, and yet it is completely delirious, it's mad. It is in this sense that we say: the rational is always the rationality of an irrational' (1995: 54).

24 This reading deepens if we consider that Roddy Piper himself left home at the same age as Nada. True, he made ends meet as a peripatetic bagpipe player, a slice of reality that seems more at home in a cult film. But it is no coincidence that both Nada and Piper found themselves on the streets at thirteen. As Piper admits in his autobiography, 'My early memories aren't … special. As a matter of fact, they're kind of shitty. To put it plainly, I was a delinquent who had a knack for finding trouble, and even when I wasn't trying, trouble found me' (2002: 2). He doesn't say anything about his parents or familial upbringing. And so the narrative of the actor's own life is also constructed by a glaring omission, at least on paper.

25 This development accompanied feminist critiques of mainstream cinema in the 1960s and 1970s: 'In 1971, 36 feminist films were produced; by the end of the decade, more than 250 were made every year. … Documentary films were prized as offering antidotes to the unreal women manufactured by Hollywood. Film scholar Julia LeSage argued that feminist documentaries incorporate the practice of consciousness-raising in their formal organization and politicize the personal experiences of women subjects they document' (Pramaggiore & Wallis 2008: 345).

26 See Tom Schatz's 'The Studio System and Conglomerate Hollywood', a chapter in *The Contemporary Hollywood Film Industry* (McDonald & Wasko 2008) for a detailed overview of the indie film movement.

27 Mutant excess erupts most purposefully in the characters of Rocky (Frank-N-Furter's 'monster', the muscled effigy of a Ken doll), 'Toxie' (nerd turned swamp-thing – heavy on the phallus) and Roark Jr. (a.k.a. the Yellow Bastard, a pedophilic serial killer who experiences certain corporeal side effects after his damaged genitals are genetically regrown). The artificial and/or deformed (but in all cases hyperintensified) masculinity of each character brings to light the social construction of masculinity and all others (e.g. femininity) that stand opposed to and are marginalised by it.

28 For me, three scenes mark the lifespan of Holly and Nada's relationship. 1) On the lam, Nada randomly kidnaps Holly in a parking garage at gunpoint, forcing her to drive him to the ostensible safe haven of her apartment. 2) Holly tags Nada on the head with a bottle of wine and pushes him through a three-story window. 3) Nada shoots and kills Holly atop the roof of Cable 54. Whatever the intricacies of their relationship, violence distinguishes its contours.

29 Both Reagan and Rose revealed homophobic attitudes throughout their professional careers. Rose's rhetoric was egregious, as evidenced by lyrics from the song 'One in a Million' on the album *G N' R Lies* (1988): 'Immigrants and faggots – they make no sense to me. They come to our country and think they'll do as they please.' In a *Rolling Stone* interview, Rose denied accusations of anti-gay sentiments while ironically confirming those sentiments. Asked if he was anti-homosexual and a proponent of gay-bashing, he replied, 'I'm proheterosexual. … I never have [gay-bashed] … The most I do is, like, on the way to the Troubadour in "Boystown" on Santa Monica Boulevard, I'll yell out the car window, "Why don't you guys like pussy?" Cuz I'm confused. I don't understand it. Anti-homosexual? I'm not against them doing what they want to do as long as it's not hurting anybody else and they're not forcing it upon me. I don't need them in my face or, pardon the pun, up my ass about it' (James 1989: 42). Reagan's homophobia, on the other hand, was distinguished by a *lack* of rhetoric with regards to the AIDS epidemic that flourished in the 1980s and almost exclusively affected gay men. Despite his silence, and his utter unwillingness to take action, it became clear how he felt about AIDS and the gay community, with conservative religio-political affiliates like Jerry Falwell saying, 'AIDS is the wrath of God upon homosexuals', and Reagan's communications director, Pat Buchanan, calling AIDS 'nature's revenge

on gay men' (quoted in White 2004).

30 In 'Grappling with Homosexuality', Vadim traces the 'gay history' of pro wrestling back to Gorgeous George in the 1950s: 'George emerged as televised wrestling's first major star. Regaled in a sequined robe, sporting artificially shaped blond curls laced with gold bobby pins, and, as announcers put it, "powdered to perfection", Gorgeous George started his matches only after a valet had sprayed his opponents with disinfecting perfume. His prissy behavior would set the standard for decades to come for the rousing of fans' homophobic jeers'. His history concludes at the turn-of-the-century with Billy 'Mr. Ass' Gunn, whose theme song reads: 'I'm an ass man / I love to pick 'em / I love to stick 'em / so many asses, so little time / I'm a lover of every kind / the best surprises always sneak up from behind.' Vadim recounts that, over the years, pro wrestling's deployment of homoerotic or homophobic antics and attitudes has been driven almost exclusively by market forces; the sexual line of flight doesn't matter as long as it spurs desire in fans and draws them to the arenas. '"Stereotypes help us bring the characters into different storylines", explains WWF spokesperson Jayson Bernstein. "I don't think we're exploiting any individual group of people. It's just a matter of entertainment." The WWF and WCW also deny purposely using gay stereotypes to encourage homophobic outbursts, but as a fan at a recent wrestling event disputes, "It's a very gay sport, and to keep it macho, homophobia must be and is incited"' (quoted in Vadim 2000).

31 The role of education and ignorance in slavery is perhaps most famously examined by Frederick Douglass in his three autobiographies: *Narrative of the Life of Frederick Douglass* (1845), *My Bondage and My Freedom* (1855) and *Life and Times of Frederick Douglass* (1892). Raised as a slave from boyhood, Douglass largely credits becoming a freeman to education and learning how to read in secret.

32 Lethem doesn't focus on mediatisation or capitalist pathology, but we reach the same basic conclusion: 'Cue mocking laughter (and an obnoxiously taunting, discofied version of the score's blues motif). We're stranded here, at the end, women handcuffed to men, in bed with the pun/chline's verdict: *We're all fucking ghouls*' (2010: 156).

33 For example, while Brandon Stroud disparages Carpenter for poor

filmmaking in *They Live*, he applauds the fight scene's hypnotic capacity, a universal reaction. According to the 240+ reviews on *Amazon*, some detractors thoroughly resent being hypnotised by a kind of hysterical ennui. An anonymous customer notes: 'The fight scene between Keith David and Roddy Piper is memorable only because it runs for about ten excruciatingly boring minutes.'

34 The tetralogy includes *Airport* (1970), *Airport 1975* (1974), *Airport '77* (1977) and *The Concorde … Airport '79* (1979).

35 In a 2005 review, Emanuel Levy writes: 'One of the most embarrassing films to be nominated for Best Picture and other Oscars, *Airport* is a trashy flick that began the cycle of disaster movies; the spoof *Airplane!* is better and more enjoyable'.

36 Most critics hold *The Sound of Music* in high regard. Some, like Jeffery Anderson, don't: 'It's a bulldozer of a musical, plowing straight through things like taste, restraint, grace, and style in favor of big, big and more big' (2001).

37 Cumbow locates nostalgia in the failure of the storyline: 'The plot-full-of-holes story idea puts *They Live* firmly in the realm of the Big Dumb Movie, the comic-book-inspired serials and programmers of the Fifties that are the film's most solid stylistic and narrative precedent' (2000: 177–8).

BIBLIOGRAPHY

Adorno, T. and M. Horkheimer (1972 [1944]) 'The Culture Industry: En-
    lightenment as Mass Deception', in *Dialectic of Enlightenment*. New
    York: Continuum, 120–67.

Althusser, L. (2008 [1970]) 'Ideology and Ideological State Apparatuses:
    Notes Towards an Investigation', in *On Ideology*. New York: Verso, 1–60.

Andersen, J. (2001) 'Totally Unprepared', *Combustible Celluloid*,
    http://www.combustiblecelluloid.com/classic/soundofmusic.shtml
    (accessed July 25).

Anon. (1999) 'Customer Reviews for *They Live*', *Amazon* (1 September),
    http://www.amazon.com/They-Live-Roddy-Piper/product-reviews/
    B0000AOX0F/ref=cm_cr_pr_hist_1?ie=UTF8&showViewpoints=0&fil
    terBy=addOneStar (accessed July 2011).

___ (n.d.) 'Keith David', *The Internet Movie Database*, http://www.imdb.
    com/name/nm0202966/ (accessed August 2011).

___ (n.d.) 'Production Notes', *The Official John Carpenter Website*,
    http://www.theofficialjohncarpenter.com/pages/themovies/tl/tlpro-
    notes.html (accessed November 2010).

___ (n.d.) 'Professional Wrestling', *Uncyclopedia*, http://uncyclopedia.
    wikia.com/wiki/Professional_wrestling (accessed May 2011).

___ (n.d.) '*They Live*', *The Internet Movie Database*, http://www.imdb.
    com/title/tt0096256/ (accessed August 2011).

___ (n.d.) '*They Live*', *Rotten Tomatoes*, http://www.rottentomatoes.
    com/m/they_live (accessed January 2011).

Bakhtin, M. (1981) *The Dialogic Imagination*. Austin: University of Texas
    Press.

Baudrillard, J. (1988) *The Ecstasy of Communication*. New York: Semio-
    text(e).

___ (2001) *Simulacra and Simulation*. Ann Arbor: University of Michigan Press.

Benjamin, W. (1969 [1936]) 'The Work of Art in the Age of Mechanical Reproduction', in *Illuminations: Essays and Reflections*, ed. H. Arendt. New York: Schocken, 217–51.

Boozer, J. (2007) '1987: Movies and the Closing of the Reagan Era', in S. Prince (ed.) *American Cinema of the 1980s: Themes and Variations*. New Brunswick: Rutgers University Press, 167–87.

Born to Controversy: The Roddy Piper Story (2006). Stamford: World Wrestling Entertainment. DVD.

Boulenger, G. (2003) *John Carpenter: The Prince of Darkness*. Los Angeles: Silman-James Press.

Caldwell, B. (1996) 'Muscling in on the Movies: Excess and the Representation of the Male Boy in Films of the 1980s and 1990s', in T. Armstrong (ed.) *American Bodies: Cultural Histories of the Physique*. New York: New York University Press, 133–40.

Christopher, N. (1997) *Somewhere in the Night: Film Noir and the American City*. New York: Henry Holt.

Colavito, J. (2008) *Knowing Fear: Science, Knowledge and the Development of the Horror Genre*. Jefferson: McFarland.

Cumbow, R. (2000) *Order in the Universe: The Films of John Carpenter*. Lanham: Scarecrow Press.

Debord, G. (1967) *The Society of the Spectacle*. New York: Zone Books.

Deleuze, G. and F. Guattari (1986) *Kafka: Towards a Minor Literature*. Minneapolis: University of Minnesota Press.

___ (1998 [1972]) *Anti-Oedipus: Capitalism and Schizophrenia*. Minneapolis: University of Minnesota Press.

Dubose, M. (2007) 'Holding Out for a Hero: Reaganism, Comic Book Vigilantes, and Captain America', *Journal of Popular Culture*, 40, 6, 915–35.

Ebert, R. (1987) 'Prince of Darkness', *Chicago Sun-Times* (23 October), http://rogerebert.suntimes.com/apps/pbcs.dll/article?AID=/19871023/REVIEWS/710230302 (accessed November 2010).

Feinstein, S. (2006) *The 1980s from Ronald Reagan to MTV*. Berkeley Heights: Enslow Publications.

Foundas, S. (2008) 'John Carpenter Lives in a BAM Retrospective', *The Village Voice* (27 August), http://www.villagevoice.com/2008-08-27/film/john-carpenter-lives-in-a-bam-retrospective (accessed June 2010).

Gould, J. (1954) 'Television in Review: N.B.C. Color', *The New York Times* (4 January), 28.

Grant, B. (2004) 'Disorder in the Universe: John Carpenter and the Question of Genre', in I. Conrich and D. Woods (eds) *The Cinema of John Carpenter: The Technique of Terror*. London and New York: Wallflower Press, 10–20.

___ (2008) 'Science fiction double feature: Ideology in the cult film', in E. Mathijs and X. Mendik (eds) *The Cult Film Reader*. New York: Open University Press, 76–87.

Gray, A. (2007) 'Top 50 Movie Fight Scenes', *Theshiznit.co.uk* (7 November), http://www.theshiznit.co.uk/feature/top-50-movie-fight-scenes.php?page=4 (accessed July 2011).

Guattari, F. (1995) 'Capitalism: A Very Special Delirium', in *Chaosophy*, ed. S. Lotringer . Los Angeles: Semiotext(e), 53–73.

Guns N' Roses (1988) 'One in a Million', *G N' R Lies*. Santa Monica: Geffen Records.

Hall, S. (2004) 'Carpenter's Widescreen Style', in I. Conrich and D. Woods (eds) *The Cinema of John Carpenter: The Technique of Terror*. London and New York: Wallflower Press, 66–77.

Harrington, R. (1987) '*Prince of Darkness*', *The Washington Post* (28 October), http://www.washingtonpost.com/wp-srv/style/longterm/movies/videos/princeofdarknessrharrington_a0aa71.htm (accessed November 2010).

___ (1988) '*They Live*', *The Washington Post* (5 November), http://www.washingtonpost.com/wp-srv/style/longterm/movies/videos/theylive.htm (accessed December 2010).

Havis, A. (2007) *Cult Films: Taboo & Transgression*. Lanham: University Press of America.

Jackson, J. (2009), 'The 30 Best Fight Scenes in Movie History', *Paste Magazine* (2 December), http://www.theshiznit.co.uk/feature/top-50-movie-fight-scenes.php?page=4 (accessed July 2011).

James, D. (1989) 'Interview with Axl Rose', *Rolling Stone Magazine* (10 August), 558, 42.

Johnston, S. (1989) 'Cheap Thrills and Dark Glasses', *London Times* (22 June), http://www.theofficialjohncarpenter.com/pages/press/londtimes890622.html (accessed December 2010).

Jurkiewicz, K. (1990) 'Invasion of the Alien Yuppies from Space: Vision and the Ideology of Blindness in John Carpenter's *They Live*', in D. Radcliff-Umsted (ed.) *Motion Pictures and Society*. Kent: Kent State

University Press, 34–40.

Kael, P. (1996) 'Raising Kane', in *Raising Kane and Other Essays*. London: Marion Boyars.

Kipen, D. (2006) *The Schreiber Theory: A Radical Rewrite of American Film History*. Brooklyn: Melville House.

Kroker, A. and D. Cook (1986) *The Postmodern Scene: Excremental Culture and Hyper-Aesthetics*. New York: St. Martin's Press.

Kwass, M. (2006) 'Big Hair: A Wig History of Consumption in Eighteenth Century France', *American Historical Review*, 111, 3, 630–59.

Larnick, E. (2010) 'Top 25 Movie Fight Scenes', *Moviefone* (28 May), http://blog.moviefone.com/2010/05/28/best-movie-fight-scenes-page-2/ (accessed July 2011).

Lethem, J. (2010) *They Live*. Berkeley: Soft Skull Press.

Levy, E. (2005) 'Critic Reviews for *Airport*', *Rotten Tomatoes* (18 December), http://www.rottentomatoes.com/m/airport/ (accessed July 2011).

Marx, K. (1878) 'Contribution to the Critique of Hegel's *Philosophy of Right*: Introduction', in R.C. Tucker (ed.) *The Marx-Engels Reader*. New York: W.W. Norton, 53–65.

____ (1978 [1848]) 'Manifesto of the Communist Party', in R.C. Tucker (ed.) *The Marx-Engels Reader*. New York: W.W. Norton, 469–500.

Mathijs, E. and X. Mendik (2008) *The Cult Film Reader*. New York: Open University Press.

Muir, J. (2000) *The Films of John Carpenter*. Jefferson: McFarland.

Mulvey, L. (2001 [1975]) 'Visual Pleasure and Narrative Cinema', in M.G. Duram and D.M. Kellner (eds) *Media and Cultural Studies: Keyworks*. Oxford: Blackwell, 393–404.

Nelson, R. (2000) '8 O'Clock in the Morning', in D. Pepper (ed.) *The Young Oxford Book of Aliens*. Oxford: Oxford University Press, 122–7.

Nelson, R. and B. Wray (1986) 'Nada', *Alien Encounters*, 6, 20–7.

Nicholls, P. and J. Clute (1995) *The Encyclopedia of Science Fiction*. New York: St. Martin's Griffin.

Penley, C. and S. Willis (1988) 'Male Trouble', *Camera Obscura: A Journal of Feminism and Film Theory*, 17, 133–40.

Piper, R. (2002) *In the Pit with Piper: Roddy Gets Rowdy*. New York: Berkley Trade.

Pramaggiore, M. and T. Wallis (2008) *Film: A Critical Introduction*. Boston: Pearson.

Prince, S. (2007) 'Introduction: Movies and the 1980s', in S. Prince (ed.)

American Cinema of the 1980s: Themes and Variations. New Brunswick: Rutgers University Press.

Ryan, T. (2008) 'Total Recall: The 20 Greatest Fight Scenes Ever', *Rotten Tomatoes* (17 April), http://www.rottentomatoes.com/m/forbidden_kingdom/news/1722234/14/total_recall_the_20_greatest_fights_scenes_ever/ (accessed July 2011).

Schatz, T. (2008) 'The Studio System and Conglomerate Hollywood', in P. McDonald and J. Wasko (eds) *The Contemporary Hollywood Film Industry.* Malden: Blackwell.

Shone, T. (2004) *Blockbuster: How I Learned to Stop Worrying and Love the Summer.* New York: Simon & Schuster.

Simon, P. (2001) 'Michel Foucault', in V. Leitch (ed.) *The Norton Anthology of Theory and Criticism.* New York: W.W. Norton, 1615–70.

Slagle, S. (2000) '"Rowdy" Roddy Piper', *The Ring Chronicle,* http://www.wrestlingmuseum.com/pages/bios/roddypiper3.html (accessed 30 June 2010).

Stroud, B. (2005) 'The 50 Greatest Fight Scenes of Film', *Progressive Boink* (30 August), http://www.progressiveboink.com/ archive/fightscenes/25–1.html (accessed July 2011).

Swires, S. (1988) 'John Carpenter & the Invasion of the Yuppie Snatchers', *Starlog: The Science Fiction Universe,* 136, November, 37–40, 43.

Thomson, R. (1996) *Freakery: Cultural Spectacles of the Extraordinary Body.* New York: New York University Press.

Thompson, G. (2007) *American Culture in the 1980s.* Edinburgh: Edinburgh University Press.

Tommy, K. (2011) '*They Live* Remake Isn't a Remake: Matt Reeves to Direct *8 O'Clock In The Morning*', *Pajiba,* http://www.pajiba.com/trade_news/they-live-remake-isnt-a-remake-matt-reeves-to-direct-8-oclock-in-the-morning.php (accessed July 2011).

Truffaut, F. (2008 [1954]) 'A Certain Tendency in French Cinema', in B. Grant (ed.) *Auteurs and Authorship: A Film Reader.* Oxford: Blackwell, 9–18.

Vadim (2000) 'Grappling With Homosexuality: Professional Wrestling – Simultaneously Homoerotic and Homophobic', *The Village Voice* (2 May), http://www.villagevoice.com/2000–05-02/news/grappling-with-homosexuality (accessed May 2011).

Weinberg, S. (2005) 'Reviews for *Airport*', *Rotten Tomatoes* (3 April), http://www.rottentomatoes.com/m/airport/ (accessed July 2011).

White, A. (2004) 'Reagan's AIDS Legacy: Silence Equals Death', *San Francisco Chronicle* (8 June), http://articles.sfgate.com/2004–06-08/opinion/17428849_1_aids-in-san-francisco-aids-research-education-cases (accessed May 2011).

Žižek, S. (2008) *Violence*. New York: Picador.

INDEX

www.ingramcontent.com/pod-product-compliance
Ingram Content Group UK Ltd.
Pitfield, Milton Keynes, MK11 3LW, UK
UKHW022258121224
452420UK00012B/577